NOT
ANOTHER

FAIRY
TALE

Cover design by: Sara Young
Cover photo by: Brianna Salzer Photography

ISBN: 978-1-957369-86-0   1 2 3 4 5 6 7 8 9 10

Printed in the United States of America

NOT ANOTHER

FAIRY TALE

FINDING FREEDOM
OUTSIDE THE SCRIPT

ASHLEY
WATTS

KUDU

This book is
dedicated
to you.
May you know that
you are seen, you
are completely known,
and fully loved.

♡
Ashley

CONTENTS

Acknowledgments ix

Introduction 11

Scene One

CHAPTER 1. Not Another Fairy Tale 17

CHAPTER 2. My Story.. 23

CHAPTER 3. Real Love 35

CHAPTER 4. Identity 43

CHAPTER 5. Forgiveness 53

CHAPTER 6. Love Your Neighbor as Yourself 69

CHAPTER 7. New Pathways... 83

Scene Two

CHAPTER 8. Teatime 103

CHAPTER 9. My Safe Haven.. 117

CHAPTER 10. Personal Healing—Personal God 133

CHAPTER 11. A New MO 141

CHAPTER 12. Contentment 159

CHAPTER 13. Joy... 167

CHAPTER 14. Come to the Well......................................171

CHAPTER 15. Happy Ending 175

Appendix A 179

Appendix B 185

Acknowledgments

God did it. He redeemed me.

I am forever thankful to be able to share this story of healing and redemption with you all.

Thank you to my ever-supportive family—I love you all.

Thank you to Becky and Heidi—Your guidance and support helped me greatly in my healing journey, and I am thankful for the knowledge and wisdom you have shared.

Introduction

The creation of *Not Another Fairy Tale* came out of the pages of my journal. Each step in my healing journey was forged through hours of counseling, prayer, journaling, and seeking God, the Healer. This book didn't start as a book. It started as a place for me to write down what I was learning about my identity in Christ, so I wouldn't forget, or rather when I did have a slight setback, I could pick it up and remind my soul of the love, truth, and hope that God has shown me. This book in no way is a step-by-step manual to healing and wholeness; there is no formula for healing—even though I so desperately wish there were a formula I could plug in and always get the same result as 1+1=2.

It's my prayer that as you read these words, you will see truth, love, and hope. If God can heal me, He can heal you too. I pray that this book acts as a soft space to land and a safe place to process your questions and beliefs. My hope is that you hear the "me too" written throughout the pages and find that you aren't alone in the struggle you may find yourself in.

This book encapsulates the steps God led me on from a place of brokenness, wrapped in codependency, shame, and loss, to a place of wholeness, clothed with newfound freedom, truth, love, and hope. The early chapters were written in the depth of my grief and sorrow as I was processing a broken marriage, a broken family, and a broken heart. Many of the chapters reflect the season I was in and the lessons and healing that God poured over and into me. God's healing work in me started at my foundation as I discovered I had lost who I was.

There are many layers to healing; head knowledge (facts) and heart knowledge (beliefs) are two. And the way to transfer head to heart is through experience. As I walked out the past few years, there were steps along the way that were just facts, things I knew but didn't truly believe or fully accept. It wasn't until I experienced God's love, grace, and comfort—firsthand—that it moved from head knowledge to heart knowledge. Experience is God's gift to us.

The second half of this book is just that: experience. Learning to love yourself, renew your mind, spend time with God, and find a new way to live and operate apart from unhealthy patterns and behaviors all take experience, trial and error, and time. The foundation is essential, but the healing really comes through experience—the experiences of getting to know yourself and the God who created you. Healing comes through relationships—relationships with God, yourself, and others.

As you journey through *Not Another Fairy Tale*, view the first few chapters as if they are explaining to you my journey to find my identity and true self. In the second half, you can see how that knowledge operates and translates into experience, where a life built with a firm foundation continues to unfold into a full and beautiful life. Just like building a home, every life needs a solid foundation. Before you can build walls, expand rooms, and lay flooring, you need to lay the foundation. If you don't, the house won't stand. If you want your house to be tall and wide, to stand the test of time, and provide shelter and comfort, you must start in the ground, and often, the foundation is the most challenging to lay.

A foundation isn't glamorous; it's all underground, deeply rooted, and unseen. It's full of dirt, concrete, and steel rods. No one brags about their home's foundation or highlights it on a home tour, yet the foundation provides the strength for the home, and this is the place true growth begins. Build your foundation, and then explore the many facets of healing God wants to bring you from there. As you build your house based on God, you will find healing and wholeness.

Peace & love,

Ashley

SCENE ONE

CHAPTER 1

Not Another Fairy Tale

We all have our version of a fairy tale or Cinderella story that we wish would happen in real life: the romance, the dream job, the adoption, or the dreamy vacation (to list a few). Life and culture have us on a cycle of posting and projecting perfection, when internally, we are desperate for rest and acceptance, always wondering if we are enough. Perfection is in our minds and hearts as something we deeply desire and want to display, but the reality is that we are human. We fall short and miss the mark, and the people we love and do life with miss it too.

We can all cut and crop our stories and lives to match Hollywood. We can crop, edit, and filter them to look glamorous and perfect, with a happy ending. Cue the music—the kiss—and the movie credits roll.

I lived my version of a fairy tale—cute plot, very little "character" development, etc. The sequence was right on, but the script was off. Missed cues and signs, more acting than real connection, my story looked good from the outside, but then life continued. Unlike the movies, life doesn't stop. Reality is there, and the harsh acceptance that we are imperfect and flawed as humans sets in. We are all people striving to portray perfection, chasing the peace we so desperately crave.

Unlike the movies, life doesn't stop.

There are rarely sequels to fairy tales, chick flicks, or Hallmark movies. If there were, the "perfect" version of love and unity would be lost in the humanness of misplaced emotion and selfish tendencies and the working out of the broken places in our lives that we so desperately try to keep hidden. Life doesn't end at the wedding, the job, or the new beginning. That's where life starts.

It took me a while to realize I was often more fixated on the "result" rather than the daily journey and the present moment. The lofty expectations I placed on people, roles, love, relationships, and life led to unmet expectations and disappointment. Resentment set in that life, people, and circumstances weren't what they should be or what I'd hoped they'd be. Perfection isn't real, and the life and love I had wanted were marred by sin, hurtful choices, and broken people.

When I thought about my life, I expected fulfillment, love, and my true identity to come from the people and circumstances around me. In my mind, I believed if I were successful enough, loved enough, served enough, and performed enough, this deep ache in my soul would be eased or satisfied. I did experience my Cinderella story as "I thought" it should go. It was all there and is documented—but Cinderella continues. What do you do when fantasy fails, and the reality of our fallen relationships rage with pain and confusion? What do you do with real life, real people, and real relationships? What happens when life is filled with struggle, pain, and confusion, and it doesn't look anything like the movie you've been dreaming up or playing out in your head?

I see you, and when I say that, I mean that I've been there—maybe not at the same time, in the same space, or through the same struggle as you, but I've been there—searching for my identity, value, and worth in different roles, positions, and relationships in which I participate. We all struggle at some point (or even many points) in life. It comes out in different ways and with different angles, views, and perceptions.

I am you; I'm human. I've been there, wondering if I'm seen, noticed, and valued. I'm the girl shyly waving her hand from the sideline, saying, "Over here . . . me . . . do you see me? Do you like me? Am I enough?" Whether you're five, fifty-five, or 105, we all have a deep longing to be seen, known, and valued. Sometimes, this need is shown through insecurities, pride, and everything in between. We want to be loved, feel loved, and accepted just as we are. The issue comes through when we search for the core of our identity, love, and security in the world, our accomplishments, or even in another human.

I've been here. . . . For. So. Long.

There has been a deep longing in my heart for many years to know that I'm significant, special, seen, valued, and loved. I have walked through the struggle of adolescents in finding my identity and worth, belonging to a group, or being accepted by friends. I've meandered my way, trying to find my identity through success and accomplishments or sports or academics. I have walked through placing my identity in my career, my job, my skills, and finally, in my marriage and motherhood. All these things in my life have been positive, but when my identity is placed there, it is quick and easy to find that it is a faulty foundation.

I have been left pleasing, earning, and striving to find my value, identity, and worth. To be quite honest, it's exhausting. I probably would have continued operating this way if it weren't for the complete shattering of the world I had created.

I found that the shattering of what I called my life and the way I found my identity was actually the sweet grace of God walking me through the fire and coming out the other side refined and changed. Let me be clear: God did not cause the fire, but He used it to rid me of chains of oppression, religion, perfectionism, codependency, poor self-esteem, poor self-talk, a critical mindset of myself and others, and a tainted image of my heavenly Father. The deconstruction of what I called my identity came in like an unwanted enemy, challenging all my beliefs, thoughts, and perspectives, leaving me torn, tired, and seeing the truth for the first time. This same breaking of me created space to see my true identity and led to finding my true self, freedom, and peace.

Life isn't what you expected? It isn't for me, either. The life I dreamed of—marriage, kids, family, house, job, and security—was shattered like broken pottery and left in a pile of shards of clay and dust, and no one was there to pick it up. I felt alone, hopeless, overwhelmed, and lost. My foundation was stripped from me, and I was at ground zero. Why would this happen? Why did I suffer this loss, grief, betrayal, and brokenness? It was in this place that truth came glaring into the broken pieces of my life, not with shame and exposure, but with love and hope. Life isn't necessarily what you wanted, definitely not like the movies, but maybe it can be more. . . .

Cue reality. Cue love. Cue forgiveness. Cue hope.

God knew from the beginning we would need love and a Savior. He knew we were human; He knew we would need hope. What if the love portrayed by culture and movies, with the expectation of fairy tale perfection, is just a counterfeit? A superficial love of perfection that derives from an unrealistic place of expectation. What if real love reaches the height and depth of both joy and sorrow, perfection and pain, doubt and hope? What if real love encompasses our desire for love, freedom, acceptance, identity, and security in a reality of an imperfect world with imperfect people? What if God knew this . . . and provided a way through Him that we can also walk in our relationships and live? What if we are actually striving for peace, not perfection? What if the love we so desperately long for is actually living inside of us—Emmanuel . . . God with us?

What happens when you are no longer striving for perfection and love from others or your accomplishments but living in the peace of who you are? What would it look like to accept God's words over you, rest in the love and acceptance of your heavenly Father, and live a life full of love? What if you were so full of love that you naturally poured love over those around you? What happens when we live at peace—loved, seen, forgiven, and whole—rather than searching, striving, or earning approval and projecting an empty portrayal of love and perfection?

Cue Jesus. Cue Love. Cue Forgiveness. Cue Truth.

The love story of the ages truly isn't a fairy tale, Hallmark movie, or rom-com with cheap love that ends where life really begins. The greatest love story ever told is the love of the God that created you, saved you, and redeemed your heart and soul.

―――――――――――――――――――――――――――――――――――

> The greatest love story ever told is the love of the God that created you, saved you, and redeemed your heart and soul.

―――――――――――――――――――――――――――――――――――

CHAPTER 2

My Story

Hi. I'm Ashley. I'm the main character in the first scene of this movie script, although most of my life I didn't act like the main character. I was trapped playing a supporting role in the movie of my life. As I shared in chapter one, I've always wanted my life to be like the movies. I wanted the fairy tale ending, I wanted the . . . *and they lived happily ever after*. I would say that this was my main goal in life, to build a picture-perfect family and live a peaceful life. The "happily ever after" I saw portrayed throughout my childhood echoed in my heart and mind and became the expectation I held. This happily ever after was peaceful and perfect. That was what I wanted. Peace.

I would seek peace the most, and perfection, which was second to peace—only by a little—also drove my actions. I felt as though if I could do all the right things and keep everyone around me happy, I'd have the life and peace that I so desperately desired. I know what you are thinking: *recipe for disaster*. And you are right. I'm not perfect, you're not perfect, and it's practically impossible to "keep everyone happy," yet that was my MO (mode of operation). After all, if I wanted my life to be like the movies, there was no room for error, imperfection, or a plot that didn't line up with a fairy tale ending.

‖‖

I felt as though if I could do all the right things and keep everyone around me happy, I'd have the life and peace that I so desperately desired.

‖‖

Playing a supportive role in your own movie isn't a good thing. It took me a while to understand that I was operating in a state called codependency. You don't know what you don't know. I had no idea that I was living a codependent life and had completely lost sight of who I was. I'm learning that part of my healing journey is having grace for myself and not judging yesterday's mistake with today's wisdom. This practice of having empathy and grace for that version of myself has allowed me to accept what *was*, process what *is*, and choose to grow and learn into who I *will* become. Let me take you to the end—which really, for me, was the beginning.

It's funny how life seems fine until it's not. It's funny when you feel like you are living for God until something rattles you to your foundation. Let me explain. I grew up in a Christian home, accepted Jesus into my heart at age five, committed my life to Jesus in middle school, and really made my faith "my own" in college. When people would ask me for my testimony, I felt silly. I didn't have a life-changing experience with God; I just grew into it. I fully understood I had sinned and fallen short, but let's be honest . . . I thought I was "good." I was thankful for God's protection, His forgiveness, and His hope. I had lived through some tough times with friendships, boyfriends, sports, job searching, marriage, and starting a family, but nothing that I couldn't handle. God felt like more of an add-on . . . to my already decided life . . . that I could "handle"—until I couldn't.

It was here, at the end (which, again, was really the beginning), that I found myself alone, broken, and shattered. Sitting in my first counseling session ever, I didn't know what to say. I had just rattled off the facts of my shattered life like they were a shopping list—no emotion and all in order. I felt numb. I had been blindsided and was in shock at what was happening to me. I didn't want to accept the fact that my marriage was shattered, trust was gone, and the fairy tale I thought I was living was a lie. I wasn't sure where to start except to tell her what had happened, and the worst part was I couldn't feel it. I had no emotion. I had lost myself.

Here I was, thirty years old, a stay-at-home mom with four kids under five years old. My twins were two months old at the time, and I was barely keeping my head above water when a boulder smashed the remaining piece of the identity I clung to—my marriage. "Someone else . . . divorce . . . only a mom . . . ," echoed in my mind as a nightmare, and I couldn't believe that this was happening.

Over the next two years, we tried to work on our marriage, and I tried to sift through the shattered pieces of my heart and find myself. What I found was that although the betrayal in my marriage hurt and caused a lot of pain, what it really did was reveal what was already there and hidden in the dark.

At the beginning of my journey, I was more concerned with how others needed to change and what they needed to do for this to work. Life wasn't changing at the rate or in the direction I was hoping for, and nothing seemed to be getting better. I kept telling God, "Please, change them. Fix them. Fix this issue." I wanted God to go back and reverse what had happened, to change it, so it wasn't real. And if He couldn't fix the past, I wanted Him to snap His fingers, change my emotions, and make it all go away. I was so concerned with how they needed to change and how they needed to act that I couldn't see my own brokenness and need for a heart change. I did know that I needed healing, but if I am honest, unforgiveness and judgment had the best of me, and in error, I thought, *I'm not the one who needs to change.*

After one of my counseling sessions, I was given the task of letting it "die." Whatever "it" was that needed to be let go of. In the session, I thought that what needed to be let go was my marriage and what I thought it was. I needed to accept the reality of what really *is*. This was something I wasn't ready to do or give up on. On a whim, my counselor suggested I drive to a cemetery and bury my false expectations and perceptions of what I was so desperately holding onto.

As I drove home, I thought it was silly. I thought, *Nope, I'll just mentally do it. I don't need to actually go to a grave and sit with this loss.* But as I drove home, I felt this deep pull in my heart to drive to a cemetery. I kept on making excuses and thought, *I'll just stop at the one by my house on my way home*, but a voice inside of me said, *Search for one here.* So, I searched for the nearest cemetery on my maps app and found Resurrection Cemetery. I immediately started to bawl. No joke. At that moment, it was as if God were promising me resurrection before I even laid anything down.

As I walked through the grass, I came upon a large cross. I knelt at the grave and started to cry again. I poured out my heart and soul to God, asking Him what it was He wanted me to let die, thinking it was my marriage or expectations of what it should be. As I was praying (more like ranting), I felt God say, *Stop . . . listen . . . I want to heal you. I want to set you free. I want you to let the old Ashley die and start your new life in Me.* I was floored. This was not what I was expecting.

Why did I need to change? Why couldn't they? I was living the best I could. I wasn't in the wrong here; they were. I was confused about what God was asking of me. I had already given my life to Jesus and asked for forgiveness; I was a Christian. Yet, there was a deep understanding that I hadn't let Christ be my Lord; I was living my life on my terms, my ideas, and my ways. Sure, I was operating with Christian morals and trying to follow God, but I hadn't truly surrendered my heart. I hadn't truly been honest with myself, let alone God. I saw that God wanted to come in, to break the barriers I had built to protect myself. He wanted to be close. He wanted to love me, but I had constructed so many walls that nothing good or bad could come near me.

I knew about God, or so I thought. However, I truly didn't know Him. What I thought I knew ended up portraying God as a distant authority figure who was disappointed in me, and that, my friend, is the farthest from the truth of who God really is. I started to see that I wasn't in a true relationship with my Creator—I actually didn't know how to be. I was a Christian and "saved," but I wasn't growing and changing to look like love, and I wasn't becoming like Him. It was as if, in a moment, God showed me my life, but from a perspective that I had never seen before. My life flashed before my eyes like a movie. . . .

I saw a young girl struggling with identity, wanting acceptance from friends and family. Afraid to make a mistake and afraid to stand up for anything, I lived limited by the confines of fear and rejection. Humility, in my mind, was cutting myself down to not appear to be arrogant. My self-talk was more of rejection. My means of acceptance were people-pleasing, indecision, and hiding my true self to not stand out. Don't get me wrong. I had a good life. For the most part, I was happy and still participated in activities and life. I had a loving family and great friends, yet I never fully showed my true self, and this deep fear in me found ways to grow as I got older.

I learned to go along to get along. I often mirrored those I was with to be accepted. I was afraid to stand out and be different. I was afraid to be myself. You might be thinking, *Yeah, me too. Isn't this what middle school and high school are like for everyone? Time to find who you are, fit in, and make friends?* I'd agree with you, yes. Yet, I never got off that train. I continued into college and adulthood, believing that my value and worth were tied to what others thought about me, how I performed, and what I looked like. I so desperately tried to be perfect and look perfect—all while rejecting who I was and trying to stay hidden.

You would have never known from the outside that I was struggling with confidence and identity. I was a straight-A student, captain of my sports teams, and student council president. I had a loving family and wonderful friends. My life was good, and I actually enjoyed a lot of it. The issue wasn't my life—it was how I interpreted my life. I thought if I lost a game or got a poor grade that I didn't have value. If a boy broke up with me in high school or didn't want to date me, I thought there was something wrong with me. I'd try to fix myself. I'd be prettier, skinnier, or funnier, so they'd want me. Others' opinions and actions determined my value. And when they liked me, it worked. It was wonderful. When they didn't, I was left at the mercy of my false interpretation and rejection. The same was true in college, so I'll spare you the details.

Taking these traits into adulthood and marriage, I was unaware that I had developed unhealthy patterns and ways of interacting with others.

The thing about codependency is that it works. If it didn't work, then fewer people would operate that way. Codependency works until it doesn't—until you get burned by it. After all, it masks itself as helping others, serving others, putting others' needs before your own, humility, and kindness. Who would call that unhealthy?

This movie continued, and I saw myself in my thirties, married with four children, and wrapped in codependency. I idolized the words of my husband, good or bad, over the words of God. I had lost sight of God; I was depressed, stressed, and exhausted. I had lost myself.

Walking through my life, I never felt as though I was scared, but I feared rejection and abandonment. To put it lightly, I wanted people to like me. I wanted people and friends to accept me. I wanted love. You might think, *Yeah, me too. Isn't that normal?* Yes. It's normal to want acceptance, to want friendship, and love. But when that desire starts to control your life and your choices, and fear jumps in the front seat, it's not normal. It's a problem.

I remember feeling that if I made a mistake, there was something wrong with me. I took criticism and rejection as reflections of my identity and worth. In adulthood, when I experienced rejection, I would again think, *Why don't they love me? What is wrong with me? Am I unlovable?* How people treated me or what they said about me became my identity. As I went into marriage, I thought I would lose friendship and love if I didn't please others. Because of my skewed view of humility, I didn't think I could like and value myself. I thought I had to deny or hate myself, and I needed other people to label me as "worth it." I became a slave to people's words, pleasing, helping, and agreeing (because that's godly, right? Nope!). And I did this in the name of my own safety and need for acceptance. Self-oppression locked me in, and my mind couldn't even connect that this was toxic.

At this point, where God led me, I saw I was a failed human, but more accurately, a hurting human. My self-effort had gotten me more wrapped up in pain, shame, and sin. Sure, some things I was doing were right, but the motive was wrong. My heart was off. I was looking to earn love and acceptance from others and the world. And to be honest, in this place of brokenness and betrayal that I had just walked through, I believed the harsh, hurtful words that were spoken over me by others. My value and worth were "owned" by others, and the worst part is . . . I freely gave it to them. People and their opinions became my idol—the basis for my emotional well-being and my identity.

I saw it.

I needed a new life, a new way of thinking, new patterns, and new behaviors.

I didn't want to live this way any longer. My joy, hope, value, self-worth, and happiness were all tied to other people. This was not a safe place for my identity, worth, hope, and joy. It's shifting sand.

So that day in the cemetery, as the rain began to fall, I laid it down. I buried my old self. I literally knelt on the ground with tears in my eyes and rain all around me and asked God to make me new. I laid down my idols of people, their words, and affirmation, and I gave God His rightful place in my life. Resurrection Cemetery . . . even before I lay down my life, it was as if God had already given me His promise of resurrection and new life. I felt different and new. I wasn't sure where to start or what to do, but God was faithful to meet me there and walk me forward.

Maybe you are in that place, too. Maybe you see the need for a new life and a change to the way you operate. When you are ready to do the same, He's there waiting for you. And friend, let me tell you—He is kind, loving, and faithful.

What God has so lovingly shown me is that He is my Creator, Savior, and Sustainer. He is the only one who has the authority to give me my value and worth. And He calls me His own, loved, chosen, and His daughter. He is my God, the solid rock, the One who paid for my identity, worth, and value. He is constant, loving, and true.

He is the solid foundation my heart yearns for, and what I have found is that He is the love I've always wanted and the truth of who I am. And God was out to change me, to make me new: a new place for God in my heart, a new identity, new habits, a new way of relationship, and a new way of seeing myself. God loved me as I was. He met me in my brokenness and forgave me all in a moment. Then He started the process of "reteaching" me who I really was. I'm learning who He is and who I am, all based on love—not judgment and perfection but truth laced in love and compassion.

This process has taken work. Some days, it's a struggle, but the self-awareness and process of healing are beautiful and messy all at the same time. I muddled through the dirt for so long that it felt as though some days I took two steps forward, and other days I took three steps back and one to the side.

I had a lot of old habits that needed to be broken and patterns of thought that needed to be lit up with the truth. I'd like to say that the "old self" never comes back, but occasionally it does, and at these points, I remember what God has so lovingly shown me. I remind myself of the truth and begin to create new habits, neural pathways, and ways of thinking. I can let go of the old, realizing these old patterns and beliefs don't serve me any longer, and I hold onto truth, to who I am . . . to who God says I am. I am a new creation made in the image of God. God is transforming me into His image, into who He created me to be.

To say I don't have a testimony is no longer true. I have been changed and made new. I have been set free and loved by the God who created me. The exciting thing is God continues to make me into His image. I'm growing and changing, and new life is springing forward every step of this journey.

I'm 4 1/2 years past the shattering news. To be honest, I didn't think I could make it four months, yet here I am, stronger than when I started. Life looks different. I'd like to say that everything was fixed, and my marriage was put back together, but it wasn't. After more hurt and truth revealed itself, I walked through a divorce. God didn't fix my life in the way I thought it needed to be fixed. I see now that if He had, I would still be in the same unhealthy patterns of codependency and misplaced identity that led me to the shattering. God did more than I expected. He helped me find the love I'd always wanted, and He helped me find ME.

Life doesn't look like I'd hoped. From the outside, it still looks a little broken and disheveled. It's nowhere near the fairy tale picture or the house with the white picket fence, but on the inside . . . on the inside, it's filled with life, love, and hope! Reality isn't what we create our life to look like from the outside. Reality is the deeply hidden parts of our lives, the true consistency of our relationships, bodies, souls, and spirits. Today, I can say that I'm happy. I like my life. Am I happy that I walked through that trial? No. It was costly, but I'm sure glad for how God brought me through it. I'm thankful for the healing I've received and the lessons I have learned. I'm whole, healed (and still healing), and loved fully.

||||||||||||||||||||||||||||||||||||||||||||||||||||||||||||||||||||||||||||||||||||||||||||||||

Reality is the deeply hidden parts of our lives, the true consistency of our relationships, bodies, souls, and spirits

||||||||||||||||||||||||||||||||||||||||||||||||||||||||||||||||||||||||||||||||||||||||||||||||

Friend, I tell you all of this to let you know there is hope. Whatever that circumstance is for you, don't give up. God is faithful. I want you to see the "me too" in this, that if He can do this in me, He will do it for you. God is faithful. For this, I am thankful. To me, this acceptance felt like the end, but this, my friend, is actually where the story really begins.

Come with me on the rest of this journey of healing.

CHAPTER 3

Real Love

There are counterfeits of love everywhere. No matter where you look in culture and in life, people, things, status, success, and much more claim to give you the value and love that you want. Relationships, possessions, and status all promise to fulfill you, but ask anybody who's gotten there—wherever "there" is—and they'll tell you that it's empty. Or even worse, what they'd worked so hard to attain was lost, stolen, broken, or removed in a blink of an eye.

Now, hear me: Relationships, friendships, marriages, kids, careers, homes, and possessions are all good. They were created by God. They are truly a gift when they are placed in the correct order in your life. *They just aren't God.* They can't take His place, nor do they fill you with what you long for.

Here is a great example of what I mean. I went to the grocery store one day at a time when I was eating mostly meats and vegetables and trying to make a healthy lifestyle change. I was walking down the frozen food aisle because I really wanted pizza. Pizza is my go-to, my love language, comfort food, the food that I would eat for the rest of my life if there were only one food I could choose. So naturally, after a few months into this change of diet, I was looking (panicking) for something that was "healthy-ish" and mimicked pizza. I found a cauliflower

35

pizza, which was good, but not the same if we're being honest. Anyway, I checked all the boxes; it was vegetable-based with meat and cheese and very little grain. I could finally have what I wanted—pizza! I could finally taste what I wanted—pizza!

As I was looking through the options, I froze! There in front of me, I saw a meatless, dairy-free, gluten-free, pepperoni pizza. Let's stop and think about that. (Pizza is gluten, dairy, and meat.) You can't tell me there's any way that a meatless, pepperoni pizza with dairy-free cheese and a cauliflower crust tastes anything like the real thing. I almost laughed when I saw it. And I very clearly heard God say, *You're trying to find a counterfeit love just like this pizza. If you look—you'll find it. It's out there, but it won't taste like the real thing. You can have it, but it won't be the real thing. And it will cost you twice as much.*

Wow! That stopped me in my tracks and 100 percent resonated with my heart and the love that I was seeking. It's the same for food and love; if you eat gluten-free, dairy-free, or any of the allergen-free options that are out there, you know those products cost twice as much and don't taste even half as good. I know it's debatable how healthy pizza is, but you get the illustration. You'll pay twice as much for a counterfeit pizza that doesn't taste or feel like the real thing, and that's the same for love.

We're all out here chasing after this great love and deep satisfaction that we truly want. Love is great, and love between people is a real thing and beneficial, but it's not something that will satisfy our soul; it's not something that will fill that empty hole inside each of us that's only designed to fit God's love.

II

we're all out here chasing after this great love and deep satisfaction that we truly want.

IIIIIIIIIIIIIIIIIIIIIIIIIIIIIIIIIIIIIIIIIIIIIIIIIIIIIIIIIIIIIIIIIIIIIIIIIIIIIIIIIIIIIIIIIIIIIIIIIIIIIIIII

You might find a counterfeit love, and it might work for a while. Relationships, food, work, hobbies, and possessions can fill that place for a moment; believe me, I've tried. And if you are honest, you have tried too. But people, careers, and hobbies were never meant to fill, sustain, and name you. In the end, you realize that you are left emptier, lost, broken, and yearning. Finding value in people, relationships, careers, hobbies, or things drives you to work, earn, please, and ultimately lose yourself to attain something no one really has. It ends up costing you too much—sometimes even your whole life.

I've lived here off and on for most of my life. With a misconception about humility and self-worth, I spent most of my adult life trying to work, earn, and please others to gain my value and worth. I willingly gave others the power to name me. I was trapped in a cycle I didn't even realize—a cycle of codependency. Codependency is an excessive emotional dependence on someone else. To say that I lost myself is an understatement. I became a pleaser to a fault; I thought if I just gained my husband's or friends' approval, then this longing to be valued, seen, and known would be satisfied. I said yes when I meant no, and resentment built. I silenced my God-given voice and perspective to not "rock the boat."

I lost all the autonomy that I once carried, thinking "sameness" would connect me to those in my life. Fear of rejection roared loudly in my brain, and my desire for love and acceptance drove me to the end of myself. Ashley was nowhere to be found. The more I worked to earn love, the more lost and exhausted I felt. I traded God's words over me for the words of broken people. I was labeled unworthy, unwanted, not enough, and only a mom. The scary thing is I started to believe those lies. Maybe you have, too. The words and experiences that have hurt us can also limit us, trapping us in cycles of depression we can't find our way out of. I longed for people and my roles as wife and mother to fill the deep chasm of my soul. I yearned for my identity, worth, and value to be recognized. The truth is that they could never fill the void I felt.

Maybe you've been there, too. Maybe you've found yourself in a season where life isn't what you thought, not what you hoped, and quite honestly, the opposite of what you desire. If that's you, I want to say, "I get it." It's a hard reality to acknowledge and an even harder one to accept. You are brave. Seeing reality and evidence of misplaced truth is challenging, and I want to tell you that you are courageous. Dictionary. com defines courage as "the ability to do something that frightens one" or "strength in the face of pain or grief." Courage doesn't mean you don't feel fear or pain. It means that you stand in the face of it. My friend, you are courageous. You are standing in the face of disappointment and loss, and the good news is, you are not standing alone. God is with you; He is the rock on which you stand. He is the One who can fill your soul and satisfy your deepest longing.

Trying to fill your desire for love and longing with people or earthly things is like trying to get a rooster to lay an egg. You can choke it, squeeze it, and wait as long as you want, but that rooster will never lay an egg. It's not in him. We do this same thing to people, jobs, children, and possessions. We try to choke or squeeze our value, worth, and love out of someone or something that doesn't hold the power or ability to name and value us. People didn't make or create you; they definitely should not have the power to name you or assign your worth. People can't satisfy your soul and longing to be loved the way your soul desires. It's a God-shaped space in you, and He is the only one who can fill you to overflowing. If you try to squeeze your identity out of others, you will frustrate yourself and them. Or worse, you will give up your value and worth to broken people with broken views and opinions.

You'll allow yourself to be named by your experiences (failure or success), and if you live by those broken people's words, you die by their criticism. People and failure can own you, and that is a scary place to live. Getting your value, love, and worth from broken people or this ever-changing world is an uncertain and risky way to live. If you haven't experienced it, take my word for it. People, careers, status, or positions can't name you, and if you do get your identity there, it's costly. The only one who has the power and ability to name you is the One who created you. This is the only safe place to land your identity, worth, and love.

The beauty of the love that God offers is that it's free. It's amazing, and it doesn't cost you anything. It's real, it's a gift, and it's free. It's called GRACE. God's love for you is unconditional. His acceptance is unequivocal. His forgiveness is undisputable. This is truly what my heart desires and only God can offer.

And yes, if you're wondering, yes . . . I did buy the pizza. It wasn't the meatless, dairy-free one; it was just a cauliflower crust. I wanted all the meat and all the dairy. Did it cost me twice as much as a regular pizza? Yes. Was it half the size? Yes. Did it taste as good? Not a chance. I won't say that cauliflower is the next best pizza crust; there's nothing like the real thing.

Now, let's get this straight; love between people is real, healthy, and good. Love is meant to be shared; we're meant to connect and be intimate with our fellow humans, but these people are also human and a limited source. We do give and receive in relationships, and that is very important—an integral part of the human experience. BUT . . . people are not meant to be our source; no person or thing is meant to be your god. Take a moment to let that register. No person, role, position, or possession should be able to have that amount of power over us or that amount of responsibility for us. That's too much weight for one person or thing to carry. We were made to be responsible TO people, not FOR them. We're meant to share love, give, and receive with the abundance of the love we already have from God.

God's love gives us identity, value, worth, and purpose. Love toward and between others should reflect this same love of God—but people can never and should never become our God. That is called codependency, and that is a very harmful and unstable place to live. When you give up your value, worth, and "lovability" to others or circumstances, they begin to "own" you. God never meant it to be that way; He wanted you to live in freedom. He wanted you to find your value, worth, and identity in Him only. Then, from a place of already being loved and accepted, you can partner with people to share, support, and love others.

The difference between the two loves is the same—it's God—but it's the order that matters. The love of God as Creator, Savior, and King, gives you your identity, value, and worth. This love gives you purpose and peace—it settles your soul. The love we share between husband and wife, friends, children, and in a relationship does not name us but shares the love we have already been given. It's a partnership, friendship, love, care, and intimacy. It affirms what God has already said about us. It doesn't act as a god over us.

||||||||||||||||||||||||||||||||||||||||||||||||||||||||||||||||||||||||||||||||||||||||||||||||

The difference between the two loves is the same—it's God—but it's the order that matters.

||||||||||||||||||||||||||||||||||||||||||||||||||||||||||||||||||||||||||||||||||||||||||||||||

The question I needed to ask myself was, *What is the motivation behind my relationships, roles, and positions? Am I looking to fill myself with the love of others or success? Or am I, out of a place of being fully loved by God, moving, living, and loving out of His abundance?* This was the beginning of transforming my mind, will, and emotions.

CHAPTER 4

Identity

I started to realize that I was in a new space, internally, in many areas of my life. Life looked different, I was different, and God was calling me to this new journey of identity, a place of peace and discovery of who He is and who I am. This was new ground, and honestly, I felt like I was standing on a cliff that was circular; it wasn't attached to anyone or anything. I felt alone and isolated, unsure where to go, what to do, and how to start.

My beginning place for searching for identity was going back to what I knew. I knew I needed to start at the ground level, sift through the pieces and shattered places of my life, and try to find out what stayed and what went. As I mentioned before, a lot of the ways I was acting and behaving in my life came out of broken places of false beliefs or misplaced truths.

Early on in my life, I learned the foundations of faith—which I am very thankful for. But I also learned a lot of cultural and religious expectations that made me believe I had to be perfect to be loved. I thought if I made the "right" choices, performed well in school, succeeded in sports, watched the right movies, and read my Bible daily, people would love me more, God would love me more, and I would be enough. I knew God's love was about grace (free love), not works, but I didn't operate that way. I had to decide and really weigh my beliefs. What was true? What wasn't true? What did the Bible say? And did I actually believe and operate my life according to these beliefs?

||||||||||||||||||||||||||||||||||||||||||||||||||||||||||||||||||||||||||||||||||||||||||||||||||||||||||||||||||||

What was true? What wasn't true? What did the Bible say?

||||||||||||||||||||||||||||||||||||||||||||||||||||||||||||||||||||||||||||||||||||||||||||||||||||||||||||||||||||

Honestly, this was a shaky place to stand. It was very uncomfortable, and I didn't like looking in-depth into my beliefs and upsetting my foundation even more than it had already been. It was scary to look at the foundation that I did have and question it, but I believe that's exactly what God was asking and inviting me to do. He wasn't afraid of my questions; I was the one afraid of them, and He wasn't afraid of the emotions and thoughts that came with the questions.

I wrestled a lot with, *Why didn't God do what I wanted Him to do? Why didn't He save my marriage? If He is a good God, then why did this bad thing happen to me?* Maybe you have some of these same questions. I had to confront misconceptions I held about God, religion, and the world. I wondered, *What does it mean to have free will? What actually is love?*

It was in this place of questioning my beliefs and thoughts and being comfortable with uncertainty that my foundation began to strengthen, not because I had all the answers but because I was willing to ask questions.

Throughout this time, I read a lot of books on identity in Christ and on healing and wholeness. I started sifting through the contents of these books and the Bible verses I grew up on and began to see them through a different lens. I began to see the reality of the world we live in, who God is, and who He made me to be. To put it straight . . . I broke up with idealism and the fairy tale I thought life really was.

I don't know about you, but I didn't love this process. I was afraid, afraid of being wrong. Afraid of believing something that was wrong. I was still caught up in the idea that there is one right way to live, one right way to process, and one right way to experience God and faith. I was stuck in the pattern of "religion" instead of "relationship" with the Creator. The shattering of this false belief allowed me to experience the freedom of being who I am, and getting to know God who created me in a way that was outside of the structure culture and religion gave me.

God began to reveal different parts of my identity and who He made me to be, through unconventional ways. Through the eyes of my children, I learned what it meant to be loved unconditionally. I saw what it looked like for someone to love you for who you are and not what you do.

As I began to be vulnerable with my friends and family about the trials I was undergoing and the challenging aspects of my life, I was met with acceptance and compassion, empathy, and love. In the past, I was so afraid of being judged that I never shared the truest parts of myself. But when I ultimately did share my brokenness, I wasn't met with judgment; I was met with love. I saw that I was missing out on the beautiful gift of friendship and vulnerability with close friends and safe people.

Through sharing the broken pieces of my life, I learned what it was like to be accepted as I was, to be loved fully, and to not have to perform. God was redeeming the places of my heart and soul, not just with my relationship with Him but in my relationships with others. It was surprising to me, too, that when I took the first step and began to be vulnerable, other people did as well. I ended up making a couple of friendships in this process that might not have been started without openness, acceptance, and love.

I'll be quite frank. If you haven't felt it yet, rewriting my identity and rediscovering God's love for me felt a little unnatural and uncertain. There were ups and downs, twists and turns, and sometimes it was hard to understand how to place my identity in God, whom I couldn't see. I questioned if this God, who I was told wanted a relationship with me, would really manifest Himself and show up in real life. Would He talk to me? Would He fill my need for a friend? Would He actually fill my heart with love? I understood a lot of the Bible and what it says about God's love for me, yet I had never let it truly into my heart. I'd never let it seep into my soul and saturate my being.

I'd like to say that my identity flourished and developed quickly, but it didn't. It took time. I began searching for who God says I was in the Bible. I wrote down verses and processed through writing what it meant to be loved, chosen, accepted, and safe. What did it actually mean when the Bible said I was a "child of God," "filled with the Holy Spirit," or "loved with an everlasting love"? I wrote and journaled short phrases . . . sentences . . . which eventually turned into this . . . the book you are reading right now. Every time I had a low point and felt emotionally exhausted, I would pull out these verses and remind myself of who God says I am.

Often in daily life, I waited for circumstances, people, or my kids to direct the atmosphere, my day, how to feel, who to be, and what to do next. A few months after my world was shattered, I was on the phone with my brother, and he shared with me something that greatly shifted my life. He described a habit that he does daily. He writes three things down in a journal every morning to remind himself of who he is. He encouraged me to not let my current life circumstances, the world, or anyone else tell me who I was. He encouraged me to wake up and choose the statements I wanted to believe, write them down, and speak them out loud over myself until I really believed them.

As I began this practice each morning, it started with three statements: I'm loved, I am chosen, and I am wanted. I had to remind myself every day that God wanted me. My family, my friends, and my children wanted me. I was loved—fully loved—just as I am.

To be honest, it sounds like a very basic place to start. But that's where I was. After everything that had happened in my life, I didn't feel loved. I didn't feel wanted, and I did not feel like I was worthy. Slowly and surely, as I continued to remind my soul each morning when I woke up of these truths, I started to believe them.

As I continued my search for identity, the statements changed to reflect what I was learning and what God was revealing about who He says I am. In the back of the book, in Appendix A, I have a list of the statements and verses of identity in Christ. You can reference that as you begin to look at yourself and what you base your identity in. This is not an exhaustive list, but it helped me jumpstart my identity based on truth, on Jesus, and on love that can never be removed or changed.

Tandem to finding my identity in Christ, I was encouraged by my counselor to find out who Ashley was, to rediscover myself, or perhaps, to meet myself for the very first time. Yes, I'm loved by the Creator of the universe. Yes, I'm chosen . . . forgiven. Yes, I was created on purpose and for a purpose, but who was I? Who did God make me to be? Those are deep questions, and truly, I didn't know where to start. Maybe you are thinking the same thing. Maybe you have lost yourself or part of yourself. Maybe you knew yourself at one point, but after all of life and all the things you've been through, you find you're in a place or in the season of not knowing who the person is that's looking back at you in the mirror. That was me; that's where I was.

I began simply by going to the grocery store and picking out food that I liked. Not food that was practical, not food that was for my children or my husband to eat—the food that I liked. This was actually more challenging than I thought it would be. Every pull inside of me wanted to pick food for my kids or my husband or find something neutral that everybody would like. My mind went to restricting myself to cost or nutritional value. I ended up leaving the grocery store with olives, sharp cheddar cheese, and tortilla chips.

You might be laughing, and at this point, 4 1/2 years later, I'm kind of chuckling at myself. To be in a place where I didn't know who I was or what I wanted, it's something that almost seems foreign to me now. This development of my identity and who God made me to be came slowly, and over time I found myself laughing and dancing with my kids, singing at the top of my lungs in the car, and finding out what I love to do in this free time that I didn't expect to have. I went out to dinner with my sister and friends, and I started kickboxing and exercising consistently. I figured out that I truly loved reading and devoured novels left and right. When the pandemic hit, stuck in my home with the rest of the world, I'd FaceTime with my friend, and she'd give me cooking lessons via video chat. Little did she know she was helping me find myself again.

Finding myself left me a little uncertain. After all, this was new, and it felt that way, and yet it also became fun. It was kind of like dating myself, figuring out what I liked and didn't like. I had to decide how I liked to spend my time. I needed to be reacquainted with my emotions, which I'm still learning to do, and honestly don't love. But even in the challenging parts of healing, like feeling and experiencing emotions for me, I'm learning to embrace that I can feel both joy and sorrow, happiness and pain at the same time. I began to see that life isn't black or white, either-or; life is full of choice, freedom, color, and perspectives, and I wanted to see myself that way as well. Identity and self-discovery are parts of a continuous lifelong journey of maturing and continuing to be reshaped.

Maybe you're there too. Maybe you don't know who you are. Maybe you do. Do you like coffee or tea? Are you a morning person or a late person? If you had free time on the weekend, what would you do? What are your hopes and dreams? What gets you up in the morning? Where do you want to be? What do you want to do in your life? What's important to you? I have been starting to ask myself these questions, as well as asking myself what God has gifted me with. What are my strengths? What are my weaknesses? Where do I feel led, and what do I feel like my purpose is?

These are all big questions and can feel overwhelming. I don't have all the answers to them, but I'm taking small steps in the direction I feel led and called. That, my friend, is growth. Take the small steps, and ask yourself the tough questions. You might not have all the answers, but you'll be closer to becoming you as you are open to questioning. Do I ever think I'll arrive and have it all figured out? No, I don't. Honestly, we never arrive. The journey continues. There's always more to learn about myself, God, and others. Yet I can truly say I'm starting to know who I am, and I'm excited to meet the me that God made me to be.

As I began thinking through these questions, I reestablished my identity and self—created boundaries and felt safe again. As I began to make choices on what I do with my time and what I would eat, believe, and think about myself, I started to gain clarity, and the resentment and anger I felt began to leave.

Identity is something I think that we as humans will always grow in, struggle with, reshape, and reform as we walk through life. It's easy to let things like culture, jobs, relationships, or roles determine our value. It's easy to find our worth there, but it's not a safe place to keep it. Yes, my role as a mom, teacher, and writer are all parts of my identity, but they're not the foundation of it. They're not where I find my value and worth. The roles and positions I have are where my value and worth go to shine after I know who I am.

|||||||||||||||||||||||||||||||||||||||||||||||||||||||||||||||||||||||||||||||||||||||||||||||||||||||||||||||||||

Identity is something I think that we as humans will always grow in, struggle with, reshape, and reform as we walk through life.

|||||||||||||||||||||||||||||||||||||||||||||||||||||||||||||||||||||||||||||||||||||||||||||||||||||||||||||||||||

Being a mom, spouse, brother, sister, counselor, preacher, teacher, or anything in between are all roles and jobs that are good, healthy, and often God-given. But they're all things that shift, move, and adjust over time with loss or change of life.

I'm finding that the core of me must be based on God. It has to be based on something that's outside of time, outside of change, and outside of this world. With the core of that in my heart, knowing that I am loved, this allows me to be free ... vulnerable ... who God made me to be, without fear of rejection ... loss ... and change.

Discovering your identity means getting into the dirt, looking and sifting through the self you have built and rely on. It means looking through your thoughts, your beliefs, and what you think about yourself. It means considering what you think about God and weighing the beliefs you operate in against the truth. Questioning is an important part of the identity process.

I found that what was normal or felt normal wasn't actually healthy or beneficial. I had to break up with normal, and I had to be okay with standing on that tall cliff surrounded by nothing, attached to no one. It's in that place where I felt God allowed me to look inside, to look to Him to find my true identity, my value, and my worth because that, my friend, can only come from the inside—from you and the God inside of you, who so desperately wants you to show yourself to the world.

The greatest thing I did for myself in this healing journey of finding my identity was getting to know God and getting to know myself. As you walk, I encourage you to ask yourself questions. Seek and give grace to yourself. I feel as though my whole life, all thirty-four years, God has been with me, within me, and around me, leading me back to Himself. I've strayed so many times. I've chosen things, hobbies, and people to fill my void, and each relationship, circumstance, or thing has failed to bring true satisfaction to my core. I have found that the only true love that can fill you and satisfy your soul is the love of God. And the only person or thing that can fill your identity, value, and worth is the One who created you.

CHAPTER 5

Forgiveness

Forgiveness is such a large topic; it deserves its own chapter. (In all honesty, it needs its own book.) Forgiveness is a gift from God to us, a generous act of love and grace that I am so thankful for, but it was never meant to just stop at us. Forgiveness is meant to flow to us and then through us, like air passing through our lungs, freely moving. I love the idea of forgiveness when I'm receiving it, yet if I'm honest, I have a huge resistance to it when I'm asked to extend it. I have found in my healing journey that forgiveness is a large portion of moving from brokenness to wholeness. Forgiveness is simple in nature and complex in application. Bear with me as we look at what forgiveness is, what it is not, and why we have such a resistance to it.

Forgiveness is something I've come into quite skeptically in adulthood. I 100 percent knew that I needed forgiveness, but I didn't want to give it, and I didn't like what it required of me—mainly extending it to others. I found that I didn't like it because I didn't understand it. I had misconceptions from childhood that led me to see this gift as something that hurt rather than helped me. I thought forgiveness meant saying, "It's okay," "I'm letting it go," or "It doesn't matter." In effect, I didn't matter, and my feelings didn't matter. I thought it excused hurtful behavior and left me with pain and sadness.

I often thought of forgiveness as a cheap apology said without empathy or acknowledging the gravity of the situation. The dialogue went like this:

"I'm sorry; will you forgive me?"

"Yes, that's okay."

I didn't like it. What happens when it's not okay—when a boundary has been crossed, and real hurt and pain are present? Forgiveness seemed expensive to me to give out and cheap for the other person to receive.

After going through this hard season in which I needed to extend forgiveness to and ask for forgiveness from a lot of people, I started to see it differently. I read different books and studied verses in the Bible because I wanted to understand it, but I had such resistance to it. People kept saying it offered freedom, but I didn't feel like it would actually work. I thought if I didn't keep my pain close, then I would be told that it didn't matter. I didn't matter. My feelings weren't valid. I thought I'd be left behind with my grief.

I hurt myself by rehearsing the hurtful things done or said to me. I "nursed" my wound by applying toxicity to it, building resentment, anger, and hatred. My heart was getting hard, and I began being very skeptical and judgmental of those around me. My pain started to come out sideways at my kids and others. In my eyes, I was the judge and in the "right," and if you've ever been there, you'll understand that this is a toxic place to live. I wanted to be free, to be joyful again and light-hearted, but what happened in my life had cost me too much, and if I decided to let it go, I felt like I was saying it didn't matter. People would be getting away free and not be held responsible for their actions.

The question was raised, "If God has forgiven me of a lifetime of offenses, how could I continually hold this one offense (or one hundred offenses) against those who have hurt me?" This question really hit me. Why would I continually put this offense on someone, day after day, year after year? Whether they apologized or not, if I had been forgiven so much, it didn't seem fair for me to hold on to unforgiveness toward someone else. I understood what was being asked . . . but I didn't like it. I wasn't willing or ready to let go of my pain.

Frustrated with myself, I cried to my counselor, "Why can't I just let this go? Why can't I forgive and move on? I don't want to hold this and keep rehashing everything, but I just can't seem to let go." I falsely believed that I needed to hold on to the pain, and in doing so, it was like hugging a board of nails. The harder I held on, the more I wounded myself. I learned that unforgiveness was meeting some need for me, even if it wasn't healthy. Unforgiveness made me feel in control—which I wasn't—and anger gave me energy, which made me feel powerful in a situation where I felt powerless.

||||||||||||||||||||||||||||||||||||||||||||||||||||||||||||||||||||||||||||||||||||||||||||||||||||||||

The harder I held on, the more I wounded myself.

||||||||||||||||||||||||||||||||||||||||||||||||||||||||||||||||||||||||||||||||||||||||||||||||||||||||

This type of power or control would not help or heal me. It was full of judgment and bitterness. This type of control and power actually hurt me and those around me. I was adding more hurt to the mess I was desperately trying to avoid. I held on to unforgiveness until I saw that it was poisoning my own soul. In hindsight, I would have let it go sooner if I had known the freedom that goes with handing God my pain and wounds, trading unforgiveness for peace and rest.

Unforgiveness is exhausting; the more unforgiveness I held, the more energy, time, and space in my mind and heart it took. The memories and words I held against others continually flooded my mind. I would be playing with my children or out to dinner with my sister trying to have fun, but the memories and hurtful parts of my past bombarded me, and I couldn't be present with the people I was with. Unforgiveness became an addiction, and the result was that my own heart and mind became more and more bitter and hard. It's often said that unforgiveness is like drinking poison and expecting the other person to die. I had heard this before, but it wasn't until I saw the effects of this personally that I truly understood. I sat in unforgiveness a long time. I won't sugarcoat it. Unforgiveness and anger comforted me at different points. It was only by God's grace that He allowed me to see the bitterness that was entangling me.

I was out on my boat with my sister one day. We had the afternoon to ourselves, so we went to our favorite coffee shop and got salads and coffee to take on the lake. Here we were on a beautiful Minnesota summer day, on the lake, with our favorite food, and I was livid. I couldn't talk about anything other than how mad and offended I was. My sister began to tell me of a great business opportunity she and her husband had, and my response was to pick it apart and find all the flaws in it. In that moment, I felt the toxicity of my own heart and soul. I heard what was coming out of my mouth, and I saw I needed to change. I didn't like who I had become, harboring this hatred and hurt. I couldn't wait for others to change. I saw that if I wanted my life to shift, it was I who needed to change. I had to take a different approach to forgiveness and decided it was time to let it go.

Forgiveness is a gift that we have been given, and in return, we get to extend to others. It is beautiful when it's extended to us, but when we are the ones hurt, it is often painful and hard to extend to others. I often want to hold resentment, anger, and pain close because, let's be honest, if someone has hurt you, it costs you something.(This is where forgiveness starts to get tricky, and I become slightly skeptical—if we are keeping this real, which we are.) God gave us this amazing gift and told us to "forgive others as we have been forgiven." Forgiveness is not a one-and-done. It doesn't stop with me; we are asked to then give forgiveness to others.

Forgiveness is a choice and a process. It is acting in faith and obedience to God as He instructs us to "forgive as we have been forgiven." This isn't an instruction based on a disappointed God who doesn't understand. This is a command based on a deep-hearted plea from a loving God who knows the freedom forgiveness offers and the truth of healing and life that will be released as you obey and forgive.

Forgiveness frees space inside your heart and mind to allow yourself to really heal. I truly believe that without forgiveness, you can't fully heal. By forgiving someone, you actually break your tie to them and the painful experience. You give up your right to get even or be paid back. You set them free to God's perfect justice and mercy, and you give God His rightful place as judge. When you step off that high ladder of holding judgment, you can see the root of all the unforgiveness.

Picture unforgiveness as a large rusty chain attaching you to your offender. No matter how many steps forward you take, if you still have unforgiveness, you drag that experience or person with you into the present. It's constantly there in the back of your mind, reminding you of and chaining you to your past. When my counselor explained it that way, I was more willing to entertain the idea of forgiveness—not for others but for me. I didn't want to walk around attached to the events and people that had so deeply wounded me. I wanted to be free. I wanted to heal more than I wanted to be paid back (which is impossible) or get even (which only puts more pain into the situation). Forgiveness is a gift you give to others, but the person it really sets free is you.

I hope you're hearing the grit and the hardness of processing forgiveness. It's not easy. It's not light, and honestly, the pains in life have cost us a lot. It's costly but worth it. Freedom is forgiveness's reward. I'd rather be free than hold on to the trauma of my past. Forgiveness is worth it. *Forgiveness is freedom.*

The freedom and healing that I deeply desired could never come from a human being. The person or event that breaks you can never put you back together; it is not God, nor should we try to make it. The only one who could truly heal me was the One who created me. He is the one who made me, knew me, and could place the pieces of my heart, soul, and life back together in the order He originally created for me. God is the ultimate source of forgiveness and healing. He understands not only the complexity of extending forgiveness but also the pain and hurt that comes with loss, betrayal, and sin. Forgiveness is not lost on Him because He is God; it originated with Him being fully God and fully man.

It was when I saw the current state of my heart and realized, yet again, my need for forgiveness and a Savior that I was able to humble myself; I stopped being a judge over others. It was never a position God intended I hold. And in the struggle of unforgiveness, I saw the roots of bitterness, anger, and grief. I started to see that continuing in this bitterness and anger was physically and emotionally costing me more pain in my life. I was exhausted. The way of forgiveness seemed lighter, definitely more attractive than this pit of bitterness and anger I had clawed my way into. God led me to see truth and freedom by showing me how to hand my past and emotions about the past to Him, and in return, He traded me His peace."Take my yoke upon you and learn from me,for I am gentle and humble in heart, and you will find rest for your souls" (Matthew 11:29, NIV).

When I let God be God and deliver His perfect justice and mercy, then I could step down from the high place in my head and be human. I saw that my steps to healing were never going to come from someone else apologizing or fixing what was broken. The only person who could heal my soul was the One who created it.

Let's keep going with forgiveness, and I'll share a little more of my story.

Forgiveness isn't just an exchange of words; it's an exchange of debt. It's releasing someone of a debt that often can't be repaid, and some of the offenses in our lives have been costly. It goes beyond a conversation and becomes a way of being. I like to think of forgiveness as a practice, a way of life. When offenses graduate from schoolyard to adult issues, we have a much harder time moving on. Forgiveness transforms from a one-time event to a process, an area I can develop and grow in: my understanding of it, practice of it, and acceptance of it.

Forgiveness is like a muscle that we stretch and build, and much like exercising, your forgiveness muscles get sore. If you don't exercise a lot or have little experience in weight training, you might think on the first or second day after your workout that you injured yourself or did something wrong. You wake up, and your muscles ache with pain you didn't feel before working out. You might even be a little tight because when you exercise and challenge the muscle fibers in your body, they break and stretch. This is how you build muscle; you are training your body to break to grow back stronger.

If you are unaware that pain is part of the process of weight training, you might stop exercising before you see results and miss out on the growth and strength to come. The same is true with forgiveness. If you stop due to misinformation or when it feels too hard, you'll miss out on the strength, growth, and freedom available. That is precisely what forgiveness does to your soul.

Forgiveness asks you to look at the offense and offender, consider yourself and your own humanness, and offer the grace that you have been so freely given to the one(s) that hurt you. You allow the grace of God to flow through you. Forgiveness is taking yourself out of the role of judge and back to the role of a human being. It often feels like it hurts or costs too much, but it's the kind of pain, like weightlifting, that leaves you sore and a little tight but stronger and freer after.

Yes, it's a decision in a moment, but it also needs to be walked out in daily life. Think of forgiveness as a process or continuum. Where are you on the spectrum of forgiveness? In my life, as I have walked through different experiences, my "forgiveness muscle" has stretched and grown. I have felt the struggle of unforgiveness and holding fast to my pain. I have also sensed the sweet grace of extending forgiveness and finding myself freer on the other side. Give yourself some grace; don't look at forgiveness as yes/no but rather as a journey to freedom and peace.

What Forgiveness is NOT:

In order to understand what forgiveness is and truly see it as a gift, I needed to debunk lies and learn what it is not.

Forgiveness is NOT:

- » Saying it's "okay"
- » Saying my feelings and experience don't matter
- » Approving of certain behavior or viewpoints
- » Allowing someone to continue to mistreat you
- » Tolerating abuse

» Saying you must stay in a relationship or reconcile

» Dismissing your pain

» Ignoring the consequences of their/your actions

What Forgiveness IS:

Forgiveness IS:

» Cutting off ties to your offender or offense

» Giving God His rightful place as judge

» Relinquishing my "right" to get even

» Relinquishing my desire to be "repaid or paid back"

» Creating a healthy boundary for myself to be safe

» Creating a healthy boundary for myself to begin healing

» Creating a healthy boundary for myself to continue in a relationship with this person or ending the relationship

» Extending the grace of Jesus that we've been given

» Recognizing our and another's humanity

» Realizing Jesus is my healer—not the person or event that hurt me

When I see the lies that I've believed about forgiveness held up against the truth of what forgiveness actually is, I am more willing to consider and extend it. My unforgiveness had kept me trapped and limited . . . chained to a hurtful past. It had left me holding the broken pieces of my life, wishing my offender(s) would apologize and change, or God would go back in the past and change the circumstance or person.

If you know . . . then you know . . . if you wait for one or both of those things to happen, you will wait a long time, maybe even forever. I had to ask myself, *If they hurt me, do I really want my ability to be healed and set free dependent on another person, especially those who hurt me?* My answer for a long time was yes. I wanted my offender(s) to pay me back, but after a few years of seeing how limiting that was, I tried another route and went to Jesus.

||||||||||||||||||||||||||||||||||||||||||||||||||||||||||||||||||||||||||||||||||||||||||||||||||||||||

I wanted my offender(s) to pay me back, but after a few years of seeing how limiting that was, I tried another route and went to Jesus.

||||||||||||||||||||||||||||||||||||||||||||||||||||||||||||||||||||||||||||||||||||||||||||||||||||||||

One day, feeling led to let go of all the hurt, I took a white piece of paper and wrote everything I could think of—all of the offenses I was holding onto and the memories and pain that continued to haunt and drain me—in red ink. For me, red ink signified the blood of Jesus covering all this pain that I couldn't forgive on my own. I needed help. I wrote nine pages. As I wrote, it felt as though I was emptying myself of unforgiveness and pain.

I sat outside my house holding what had cost me so much emotionally and mentally the past few years, and I felt God prompt me to let it go, to burn it. Part of me wanted to hold onto those pages, to keep them close. Another part of me was curious to know if all this forgiveness talk truly did bring freedom. With some resistance, I crumbled up the papers and lit the match. I watched them burn, the red ink almost disappearing off the page, the paper turning white again right before it was consumed. It was amazing. I didn't think that the red letters would be erased by the fire, but they were. It felt cleansing and symbolic of a new start.

I handed my hurt to God and released my desire for justice, and healing began to swell. My unforgiveness had left me unable to process what was under the anger, disappointment, sadness, grief, and loss. As I lay down my resistance, my emotions and tears began to flow. I was able to name the emotions that hurt so deeply and learn healthy ways to process them. I still had anger, but that anger showed me where a boundary was crossed and alerted me to action. My tears washed my heart, and as I let the emotions flow and was honest with myself, my mind became less cloudy. I could see more clearly.

My heart began to soften, and I found peace. It settled my soul, not because anything was fixed, but because my walls had crashed down, and I could let love in. As I continued this walk of forgiveness, it was a daily choice to hand over my cares and concerns. The memories and pain didn't disappear after the one marked moment of forgiveness; it was a slow fade. Each day I'd still have triggers and memories pop up, and daily, I'd release them mentally as I did in the fire that day. I would speak the truth or say a Bible verse out loud to remind myself I was loved and safe. Slowly but surely, over time, memories began to fade, and triggers that usually bothered me didn't. My mind became less consumed, and eventually, I went a couple of days and then even weeks without the haunting memories trailing me. I began to feel free and be present in the moment I was in.

Did I forget? No, and I think that's a good thing. If I had forgotten, then what would stop me from entering the same type of situation again? It was truly a miracle—my mind and heart were being healed. Even now, four years later, I occasionally have memories pop up. I can feel the emotion, but it doesn't affect me the same way. Yes, I still don't like the situation I went through. A layer of pain sits in tandem with deep-seated gratitude for how God has healed me and walked me through.

Forgiveness can happen between two people only in a safe and healthy space. In a safe relationship, reconciliation and redemption are possible, and that is amazing. Both parties involved need to be vulnerable, willing, and open to hear, validate, and mend the relationship. I'm so thankful when this is possible. Two people can deepen their relationship and grow stronger through this process (again, like weightlifting).

Sometimes, reconciliation is impossible in a relationship due to many different reasons (death, abuse, an unwilling person, etc.), but forgiveness is still possible. Forgiveness and healing can happen just between you and God since it frees you—not your offender. Forgiveness and healing with God is saying, "I release my offender(s) from owing me anything. I give this offense and person(s) to You, God. You are a judge, and I am not. Your will of mercy and justice be done. I want healing and freedom, Jesus. I invite You to help me in this journey of releasing the hurt and pain; I know You are the healer." And then I walk forward and let the Healer lead and guide me.

My forgiveness journey started when I decided to work on what I could control, myself. I learned what I needed to become a healthy person and in turn, many skills that aided in the forgiveness process. For example, I could set boundaries to protect myself, and God started to heal my heart. I discovered what was mine to own—starting with my ability to say yes and no. I determined how I wanted to be treated, what I would allow, and what types of relationships I would participate in. This level of ownership created a space where I started to feel safe and grow in trusting myself and others.

I also learned that my emotions and experience were mine to process and work through. I could no longer place my anger on someone else and expect them to change. That is a trap that too many of us, including myself, have fallen for. My emotions were mine to deal with and no one else. Yes, that situation hurt. It shouldn't have happened, but I can't live my life based on other people. It's too risky.

I learned how to be self-aware, validate my emotions, and work through them. I learned to see my emotions as a gift and signal, alerting me to what is happening under the surface. If a light appears on your car's dashboard, you don't ignore the light; you investigate what's happening under the hood of your car. Much like the lights on your dashboard, your emotions act as signals to alert you to what's going on in your mind and heart. If you ignore your car signals or your emotions, you might encounter a breakdown.

Emotions are important and must be addressed. They are meant to help you and guide you—not drive, just like I can't let the lights on the dashboard drive my car. I control where the car goes, and it's the same with emotions. My emotions don't control me, I am in control of myself, and I get to choose how I process emotions and what I do with them. You might think emotional awareness is a basic function of life, but the more I live, the more I see myself and the rest of the adult population struggling through emotions and ways to process and guide them in healthy ways.

As I set some personal boundaries and began to own my emotions and story, I slowly started letting go of the unforgiveness and taking control of the climate in my own heart. For me, it was a slow, drawn-out process but a choice I made in a moment . . . a choice you can make now. Remember, forgiveness is a choice and a process. God is faithful. He will show you how to heal, how to forgive, and how to process. He is doing the work in you; you just need to listen and obey His loving prompts.

Where do you start? How do you start? Maybe you are thinking there is too much to forgive. Maybe you don't even know what or whom you are holding unforgiveness toward. Is it a friend or family member? Maybe it's something from childhood. Maybe you need to forgive yourself. The idea is to start small. Start with the choice to forgive. Have a marked moment of deciding to forgive, and do it today. Ask God to help you, to alert you to whom or what you need to forgive. Don't wait; freedom is on the other side.

A few ideas:

>> Begin by taking ownership of your emotions and the climate of your own heart.

>> Choose forgiveness—It's freedom and healing. God will help you. After all, He is the One who forgives.

>> Write down the list of offenses, long or short—color it red as symbolism that Jesus's blood covers the painful moments—and burn the list, or wash it in water. Process the pain, and then let it go; get rid of the list.

>> Give yourself grace. Life happens, and triggers can send you back to those hurtful emotions all over again. Place those events and cares at the feet of Jesus, and choose to forgive again. Make it a way of life.

>> Speak—out loud—a positive affirmation or a Bible verse. Fill your mind and spirit with truth.

>> After you release the unforgiveness, ask God to fill you with His peace, comfort, joy, love, truth, and grace.

>> Reevaluate or establish personal boundaries. Boundaries are meant to keep you together—not control others. Boundaries are for you!

There are many books dedicated to forgiveness with God and each other. Continue to read and process the journey of forgiveness. I also encourage you to find a Christian counselor and community that can support you on your forgiveness journey.

CHAPTER 6

Love Your Neighbor as Yourself

At many points in my journey, I believed that I was unlovable. I was unworthy of care and kindness; I thought I deserved to be treated in the unfair and unloving way I experienced. If I were lovable, then people would treat me that way, so I must not be "enough." Unfortunately, I allowed my circumstances to dictate and reinforce what I already had believed about myself: I was a burden, unwanted, and merely tolerated.

After some time of believing this, I started to see it manifest through my experiences, which then informed and reinforced my wrong belief about myself. The thought that I deserved to be treated as less than or a burden continued to grow. I was in a vicious cycle of poor self-image and poorer self-talk. What's scary is that what you look for, you will find, and I was out to prove that my haunting thoughts and experiences were somehow correct. I didn't like myself; I didn't know that I could. If others liked me, then I was okay or safe, but if they didn't, it just assured me that I was flawed and wrong.

I don't know about you, but how I often speak to myself isn't great. It's full of judgment, disappointment, and comparison. It's laced with the idea that I should look different, act different, or be someone I'm not. I think that through the process of growing up in this American culture, image-filled and filtered reality, I had the idea that there was a better way to be, and I was not it. I felt the pressure to be smarter, skinnier, prettier, and funnier. Everything that I was wasn't good enough, and adding to the mess, I thought I had to have other people's approval—not just God's and my own—to be of value. I think many of us live this way. It's natural to want approval and acceptance. It is just a risky and expensive way to live.

To me, this was normal, and I didn't really see an issue with it. I thought that's what everyone thought of themselves. If you are like me and have a lot of loud voices in your head, I want to help you notice something: the things you may be thinking about yourself might not be true. These thoughts can harm you and are informed by lies.

Tied with my mistaken philosophy that I couldn't like myself, that it was prideful or arrogant, I had to value others over myself and think of myself as nothing. Whether this was directly taught to me or was my own misconception, it's not healthy or true. Now hear me, yes, it is important to value others and think of others' needs above my own, but that doesn't mean I neglect my own needs. And it also doesn't mean that to love and value another person, I need to devalue or hate myself. There is a huge misconception about the terms "self-love" and loving yourself, and it's time we debunk the lie.

I don't have to tell you that we live in a selfish culture; I'm not advocating for being selfish. I'm saying there is a difference between being selfish and self-centered and loving yourself. Selfishness sees the needs of others and disregards them to serve one's own purpose or need. Self-centeredness doesn't see the needs of those around them at all.

Loving yourself is not selfish or self-centered. Loving yourself is self-acceptance. It's valuing yourself and how God made you. It's accepting your value from God and giving Him His rightful place of being your

Lord and Creator and agreeing with who He says you are. Loving yourself allows you to receive the love of God, love yourself, and then pour that into those around you. It doesn't make you selfish; quite the opposite, it makes you secure. It sets you on a solid foundation in Christ that allows you to prioritize the cares and needs of those around you.

If your deepest needs and desires are met through God, and you know who you are, you are then free to focus on others and add value to their lives. The comparison stops, the working and earning stops, the cycle the world has set us on stops, your soul truly settles, and you are at peace. It is in this place of peace you can serve. You can't truly love and accept others if you haven't first accepted God's love and then applied it to yourself.

Another misconception I had was I thought that I had to prove my worth to people and myself. I held the belief that I couldn't hold my own value or even like myself. I couldn't believe what God says about me. I thought humility was self-hatred, and if I wanted to be truly humble, I couldn't name myself. I thought I needed others to name me. I had a warped sense of humility which left me exposed to codependency and idolatry of people over God. This view left me working and pleased to earn my value and identity from people's opinions rather than having it rooted in God and self-acceptance.

IIIIIIIIIIIIIIIIIIIIIIIIIIIIIIIIIIIIIIIIIIIIIIIIIIIIIIIIIIIIIIIIIIIIIIIIIIIIIIIIIIIIIIIIIIIIIIIIIII

I had a warped sense of humility which left me exposed to codependency and idolatry of people over God.

IIIIIIIIIIIIIIIIIIIIIIIIIIIIIIIIIIIIIIIIIIIIIIIIIIIIIIIIIIIIIIIIIIIIIIIIIIIIIIIIIIIIIIIIIIIIIIIIIII

I would serve, work, please, and show kindness to others, not so they'd feel loved, but so they would see and name me as valuable and loveable. I was working on getting others to like and accept me because I didn't or couldn't like and accept myself. When I thought about it, I called it "Christian." I was denying myself and putting others first. The reality was that I was putting others first, hoping to find a sense of security and self-worth through them. This is called codependency.

In my case, I was depending on many people to give me emotional, mental, and spiritual stability. I depended on my husband, friends, parents, and even my children to give me value. I was operating in performance-based living, which left me anxious and exhausted, in a never-ending cycle to earn my value. When I was successful and helpful, I felt good and secure; when others were upset with me, or I failed, I thought I was worthless.

My actions became selfish in nature even though they looked like I was serving; my heart was not in the correct place. I lived like this for many years, and in participating in codependency, I was truly handing over my identity, worth, and value to another human who, like you and me, is faulted and broken. So, you can imagine, when I heard the news of my marriage ending and felt unwanted as a wife, my self-image and self-worth plummeted right alongside his words and opinions.

Humans were never meant to be God, and that's what happens when you operate in codependency; you make people your god. People are not a "good god." No one should have that ability and power over another human. After all, we are all on a healing journey to become who we were created to be. Unfortunately, you might run into some broken and hurting people who, if given the power to name you, can do more damage than you can imagine. I'm sure you've heard the quote, "If you live by their praise, you'll die by their criticism." It's true; I've lived it. If you give the power to a person, relationship, or even career, to name you, you then become enslaved to their opinion and words.

I know that sounds extreme, but it's true. As humans, we all filter through these dynamics and challenges in life and relationships, but when it becomes your mode of operating and way of finding security, it's a scary place to live. If you have had experience in codependent relationships, you know the trap I'm talking about; you might also know the pain of harmful and hurtful words spoken over you. The good news is that you have the right to call a fault—to either believe the lies or believe the truth. Codependency is a cycle that can be stopped. Hope is not lost.

Codependency can work for a while; otherwise, we wouldn't participate in it. When life is good and working in our favor, operating in codependent patterns can make us feel good . . . until you must work for the validation yet again. Working for praise and approval can give you a sense of pride and reward. It can also become an addiction, and that can become what you fill your identity with. It's dependent on your ability to perform, and let's be honest; it makes us feel like we are in control. We think we can control our future, friendships, and life. But control is not love; it is manipulation. Love is free. Control is never what God intended for us, and if we are truly honest, we have control over very little, which often gives us anxiety or stress that then perpetuates the cycle of working, earning, and pleasing others. I know just reading this, you are exhausted. Me too. There must be another way; stick with me.

Finding myself with a loss of identity and spiraling into more negative self-talk, I tried harder and harder to please others. The hard part was that no one was watching, and all the effort I was putting in to please someone else didn't do a thing. It wasn't enough. It would never be. I was on the cliff again, the one I mentioned earlier, where nothing and no one was attached to me. I had to look inside myself and see who I was. I had to face the fact that I didn't like myself. And I couldn't expect others to like me or even know me if I first didn't know and like myself. It was in this place that I had to figure out how to love and validate myself, to accept who God made me to be. Unless this happened, I'd stay in the vicious cycle of needing others to validate and accept me. This was a struggle. It felt odd, not normal, and like it wasn't okay.

I started to notice the ways I talked to myself. I was harsh and judgmental constantly throughout my day. I noticed oppression or depression in my body due to my poor self-talk. I took inventory and thought, *I'd never talk to my daughter or friend that way. Why do I speak to myself like that?* I began to have more questions, *What would it look like to like myself? Is it okay to like me? How would it feel if I called myself loved, good, worthy, or enough? What would it mean if I didn't try to constantly change myself but accepted myself for who I was?* With some resistance, I gave myself permission to like myself.

When I am not secure or don't accept who I am, I spend most of my life working to fill my own needs of love and acceptance rather than serving and loving others. I may be selfless and others-focused, but the motive is selfish. As I began to love myself, I moved out of survival mode and could be present to the needs of others around me. I could actually love others because I loved myself. This paradigm shift was life-changing. Denying myself had created an internal panic to do whatever it took to be good enough. Learning to accept God's love and love myself set that inner drive to rest and helped me to love others authentically and more fully.

My faulty beliefs—lies—had held me captive and informed my thoughts and decisions for thirty-three years, and I didn't know. A lie often looks close to the truth, just a little twisted. The other tricky part was that if I believed a lie, it would operate as truth as long as I gave it the power to. That's what had been happening; false beliefs about humility, myself, and others led me on a cycle of living a lie, and I bought into it. My counselor once told me, "You don't have to believe everything you think." This statement changed my life, and I want to tell you that too.

You don't have to believe everything you think.

You get to decide what stays and what goes. Thoughts are just that— ideas. You get to decide what to do with them. It's called mind management. The Bible talks about it in 2 Corinthians 10:5. I love how the Amplified Bible states it:

> We are destroying sophisticated arguments and every exalted
> and proud thing that sets itself up against the [true] knowledge
> of God, and we are taking every thought and purpose captive to
> the obedience of Christ.

Thoughts that run rampant in your mind can be destructive. Over time, if you don't control them, you can wind up believing the lies we hear from culture, our past experiences, or even ourselves. These lies can be deeply rooted in our brain and (spiritual) mind, and we won't even recognize them as lies. They will become a second nature "truth" that operates without our awareness. The concept of mind management and self-awareness is talked about in culture as a way to help you live in health and peace. It isn't something new . . . it originated with God. We need to think about what we are thinking about. We have to take our thoughts captive to the obedience of Christ. To say it plainly, does what you are thinking line up with what God says about you? Do your thoughts line up with truth and love? Do what you think and say to yourself help or hurt you?

It took my life and the false identity I had built to come crashing down for me to realize the pit I was in. I wasn't even aware of the lies I had believed and the way in which I was oppressing myself. It was hard to accept and realize that a lot of what I believed was hurting me. I was held captive by my own false beliefs. It was also freeing to see that I (with Jesus) held the key to my own freedom. It wasn't dependent on someone else or even on my circumstances changing; it was dependent on a loving God showing me the powers of choice, self-acceptance, and learning to love myself and the way God created me.

In the beginning, God created the heavens and earth, water and land, sun and moon, sea animals and land animals; He also created humans. Everything He made He called good. However, after He made mankind, He said something different, "And God looked upon all that He had made, and indeed, it was very good." (Genesis 1:31, BSB). He said it was *very* good. God created us in His image. Therefore, we should see ourselves this way.

Yes, I do know we are human, and we have sin, yet God created us good—in His image. We were separated from God, but being so loving, He made a way to restore that relationship. We can now be in His presence, not because of anything we have done, but because Jesus took our shame and gave us His righteousness. When God sees you and me, He sees Jesus. First John 4:17 (KJV) says that "as [Christ] is, so are we in this world." God doesn't look at us with shame and disapproval. He looks at us with love. He sees us as His children. He sees who He made us to be, and He sees His love . . . Himself in us.

One way to look at self-acceptance is to begin seeing ourselves the way our Creator does. Who does God say we are? How does He view us? The second part of this is accepting, believing, and living this truth out in our daily lives—self-acceptance.

I felt God clearly say to me one day, *Stop rejecting what I have called good.* I had finally begun to root my identity in truth, and I was starting to believe God's word over me as opposed to what others have said or my experience. Then I realized that what was holding me back wasn't others; it was my own thoughts and judgments of myself.

Through a series of sermons, books, and counseling work, I began to sit with the truth that I was ultimately rejecting myself. It's hard to say . . . to admit that I was causing this discomfort and continual pain in my life. My journey really took many steps of healing for me to even be able to see this.

If you ever have dealt with rejection, you might know this lie: It's better if I reject myself before anyone else does. Or, if I reject myself first, it will hurt less when they do it. Neither of these statements is healthy or correct. Rejection hurts, regardless of who is rejecting you. Rejection is worse when you do it to yourself. I was in this pain cycle because I was afraid of rejection. I was afraid to hope, feel joy, or think positively of myself, lest I found out I was wrong or someone took it away. Even as I am editing this book, I'm brought to tears knowing the depth of this fear and false truth. The hardest part of this cycle is that no matter how others see me or even how God sees me, I will still interpret it as rejection if I am rejecting myself. It's as if I am wearing sunglasses, and the lens I am looking through is tainted/dimmed by rejection. I can't live by others' praise or criticism, but I can accept their affirmation of who God already says I am. However, this can't happen without my first loving and accepting myself.

I'm not saying to "accept" yourself and never change or grow; that would be foolish. I'm saying to love and accept the core of who you are. Love and value who God made you to be, knowing God created you purposefully.

God created you, me, and humankind—all so different, yet all reflect His image. Often, we seek "sameness," but we were not created to be the same. We were created and knit together differently in our mothers' wombs, with love, intention, and purpose. You, my friend, are not a mistake; you are full of purpose, and so am I. Your laugh, height, personality, giftings, abilities, and quirks are God-ordained. Yes, we all have places of brokenness and areas that need healing; we live here on earth. But the core, the reality of who you are . . . is good. You were made with care, on purpose, in the image of God.

Why do we keep rejecting ourselves? In essence, when you reject, criticize, judge, or compare yourself, you are going against what God made. You hate what God created and called good. When I was honest with myself, and if you are honest with yourself, too, you can see this old way of thinking isn't helpful. It's painful; we are our own worst critics. I finally came to a place where I saw that I needed to—more importantly, I wanted to—make a change.

Mark 12:30-31 (ESV) says this:

> *"'And you shall love the* LORD *your God with all your heart and with all your soul and with all your mind and with all your strength.' The second is this: 'You shall love your neighbor as yourself.' There is no other commandment greater than these."*

God gave us two commandments (among others). The first is to love the Lord your God with all your heart, soul, mind, and strength. And the second is to love your neighbor as yourself. *This is great,* you might be thinking, *I love God with all of myself, and I love others well. I just don't know how to love myself.*

If you look closely, it says to "love your neighbor AS yourself." How can you truly love another person if you don't first know how to love yourself? This has taken me a while to really grasp. Please go back and read that again. My thought process had been, *I thought loving myself was selfish or prideful. Yes, I understand that God's love needs to fill me first. Then, the love I've received can flow to others, but I can't love myself.* This false belief had been deeply rooted in my mind.

Please stop, and see that. First, you need to receive God's love. Part of that is loving and caring for yourself. Loving and accepting yourself actually honors the God who created you. God gave us self-control, a fruit of the Spirit, and responsibility for our own hearts, actions, and selves. We are only able to love others to the extent we love ourselves. So, if my self-talk and self-perception are flawed and hurtful, that is also the lens that I will use to see others. It may look like criticism; it could look like the idolatry of others. Neither is love.

God loves you; He wants you to view yourself as He views you. He wants you to be thankful for who He created you to be. Celebrate who you are, and live fully in who you are. That is why He made you, with purpose, to serve a purpose. The world needs who you were created to be. The world is spinning for love and affirmation and acceptance from anyone who will give it to them. God is asking you to jump off this hamster wheel of striving and accept who you are. Accept His grace, His gift of Jesus, and your new identity. Accept yourself, your personality, your looks, and your mind. He created them. No one except God can give you identity, and only you can accept it for yourself.

What would it feel like to accept yourself—to stop trying to be someone different or change the core of who God made you to be? I'm not saying to stop growing and maturing. I'm saying to pause and ask the Holy Spirit, that internal voice, who you are. Ask Him how He shaped you and framed you. What would it look like to become a student of yourself? To figure out how you process and how you can thrive, to seek to understand the gifts God has given you, and then live out the call on your life?

I truly don't think we can live out our callings and, at the same time, reject ourselves. One will win, and it's not our calling. Nothing can stop God's plan in our lives but us. God won't force us to follow Him. He gave us free will, and it's our responsibility and joy to align our hearts, minds, and actions to Him. Loving others starts with receiving God's love for us and loving ourselves. This gives us the solid rock and foundation of who we are in Christ and allows us to then live out of a place of security instead of living life trying to create it.

Sometimes I wonder, *Why is it so hard to accept and love ourselves?* I think there are two reasons.

  1) It's not natural.

  2) We practice conditional love with ourselves.

Or at least I do. I hold myself to standards that I would never hold others to—standards that God never placed on us. I often demand perfection of myself and am disappointed or feel unworthy if I don't live up to the standard of perfection in my mind.

 If we practice conditional love with ourselves, we will likely practice conditional love with others. We'll hold ourselves and others to standards that God never placed on us. We'll keep operating out of patterns and learning that we have built over our entire lives, and for some of us, that's a long time. Thirty-three years of operating one way aren't changed in a day or even a week. It has been a slow journey of learning to look at myself with grace, compassion, and love. With the Holy Spirit's leading, over time, I have been able to change my thoughts . . . which have changed my patterns . . . which then changed my behaviors . . . and my life.

 Learning to love myself brought a grounded and deeply rooted presence to my life. I was able to jump off the cycles of searching for love and acceptance that exhausted me and left me in selfish survival mode.

Loving myself and accepting who I am has taught me to love others in a more authentic way. As I began to care for myself, I found that love for others was welling up in me. I was no longer a broken vase where water poured into and seeped out the cracks, leaving me searching for more love. I felt healed and whole. Where God's love and the love of my family could be poured into me, I'd "fill up," and in turn, love would pour over onto others. As I began to accept myself, even my quirks and nuances, I found myself more accepting of other people and celebrating their differences. To be honest, this level of self-acceptance and loving myself has brought true joy and contentment to my life.

How you see yourself matters. How God views you is most important, and how you view yourself is second. Our goal is to align with Him—to accept, not reject, what God has created. Begin the journey of getting to know the real you, the you that this world so desperately needs. Don't just get to know you—love you. Accept who you are and who God created you to be. It might feel odd. It did for me, too, but this is another moment where we are given a choice. Whom will we serve? What will we follow? The way it's been is no longer the way it must be.

Freedom came as I began to accept myself and love who God made me to be. We can choose our thoughts, the way we view and speak to ourselves, and God's words over us. Let the chains fall, and walk forward into truth. It's a decision to make today and a process that will continue to grow and bring you to health. Let's do this together.

||||||||||||||||||||||||||||||||||||||||||||||||||||||||||||||||||||||||||||||||||||||||||||||||

Let the chains fall, and walk forward into truth.

||||||||||||||||||||||||||||||||||||||||||||||||||||||||||||||||||||||||||||||||||||||||||||||||

You are valuable. You are loved, and you deserve to be treated with kindness and respect, starting with yourself. Know your worth, and believe you are valuable.

CHAPTER 7

New Pathways

After realizing the limiting place of self-rejection and denial I had been living in, I started to have a lot of questions about how I got there and what I should do next: How do I change? What's this process of aligning myself with who God says I am? How do I stop looking to people, roles, and positions for my value? How do I stop living based on performance? How do I truly love and accept myself?

I began to get my hands dirty and started sifting through my beliefs and thoughts. I pulled the weeds and kept the truth. I was aware that not all of it needed to stay. Not all your beliefs are true either, nor do they help and serve your purpose. It's important to look at your thoughts and beliefs against the Word of God. Do they align? Is how you view yourself consistent with what God says about you? What is informing your thoughts and, ultimately, your behaviors?

I truly understood that how God views me is the most important place to root my identity; everything else was shifting. It's the firm foundation, the never-changing rock on which to build my life. The second most important thing is how I viewed myself. You are the most powerful agent in your life. You can either accept or reject what God says about you. It's your choice. Often, though, we don't act like we have a choice in our thoughts and perceptions of ourselves. Part of re-rooting your identity in Christ is self-acceptance, learning to love yourself, creating new brain pathways, taking charge of your mind, and taking your thoughts captive.

Friend, I'd like to tell you that you are already on this journey; you're doing it. Through this book, and I'm sure in different areas of your life, you are starting to become aware of the places you need growth and healing. I'm doing that, too, and I continue to walk toward healing and health daily. I saw the need, the need for God to hold my identity. You can probably also start to see why He is the only secure place to put your identity. God is the only constant and unchanging solid rock; He is outside of time and circumstance, and what He offers is free. I'm sure you know by now, and if you don't, take my word for it; the world offers nothing free. He is the answer. I want to encourage you that you are already on a journey, and God is with you.

|||||||||||||||||||||||||||||||||||||||||||||||||||||||||||||||||||||||||||||||||||||||||||||||||||

God is the only constant and unchanging solid rock; He is outside of time and circumstance, and what He offers is free.

|||||||||||||||||||||||||||||||||||||||||||||||||||||||||||||||||||||||||||||||||||||||||||||||||||

How many of us have a Roomba or a robot vacuum? I bought a Roomba, but I didn't want to pay too much, so I got the cheap version—the version that just bounces off walls and furniture; it has no logical way to clean or move about my house. The higher-level Roomba vacuum uses a map; it takes time to chart the area, creates a map, and moves through the space in a planned pattern. It's an amazing product. This machine was made to help me and do so much, but without the upgraded system, the Roomba I bought just keeps bouncing off everything it hits. I end up babysitting my Roomba. I follow it around as it vacuums, trying to get it to go to where the mess is.

The Roomba, left on its own, gets stuck and off-track in the oddest places—I think some of us can relate this to how our brains work. We need the upgraded Roomba map. We need a new brain pathway, a new map, and a strategic way to move through our lives and circumstances, so we don't just get caught bouncing off every circumstance and tangled in old patterns of thought and behavior.

It was in this place of repeated bouncing off of everything coming at me that I saw God slowly showing me the need to have a map, a planned route, and a new pattern for my thoughts and beliefs. If you resonate with the vacuum story, then you may be thinking the same thing. God wants to give you a new map, a new grid, and an updated system. God wants to change your brain pathways to renew your mind. He wants to take the names, labels, and limits that others or even you put on yourself and set you free. He wants you to identify with what He says about you.

Romans 12:2 (ESV) instructs us: "Do not be conformed to this world, but be transformed by the renewal of your mind, that by testing you may discern what is the will of God, what is good and acceptable and perfect." And Philippians 4:8 (ESV) tells us exactly how to do that: "Finally, brothers, whatever is true, whatever is honorable, whatever is just, whatever is pure, whatever is lovely, whatever is commendable, if there is any excellence, if there is anything worthy of praise, think about these things."

Doing this took time and work. It required me to dig into some of the harder areas of my life and confront my own hurt, my own shortfalls, and how God wants to heal and redeem those pieces of my heart. This required me to be open and honest about challenging and painful experiences that have marked me and allow God to bring me freedom.

In my journey, I have found that healing takes a community. Don't dive into the deep on your own. Find a Christian counselor to walk with you through your healing journey. Find a few close friends who are safe that you can share with and lean on when times are hard. Seek out a prayer ministry (Sozo Prayer, for example) that will surround you and aid you in healing and hearing the Holy Spirit. Just don't do this alone.

I have seen a counselor weekly for the past four years. I have met with a prayer ministry and been surrounded by loving family and friends. Hear me again: find community, and if you don't have a supportive community, go to your local Bible-preaching church and get involved. Healing is a journey and a process, and a support system is so important to have along the way. Be kind to yourself, and seek healthy support and relationships.

God loves us as we are. He accepts us as we are. Yet because of His love and grace, He doesn't leave us there. It's like the love of a parent for their toddler. We love them fully and wholly where they are, but because of our love for them, we teach them, help them grow, and guide them. To leave a toddler as they are forever would be a disservice to that child. They would be a thirty-two-year-old who still behaves like a two-year-old. God loves us too much to leave us in the lies, misconceptions, and false beliefs that come with living here on earth. You can know the truth and be filled with the truth, but you can't hold the truth if you're full of lies.

In my experience, God starts with love. He teaches us who we are and our value. Then, He graciously shows us the truth and the ways in which our false beliefs aren't serving us but hurting or even oppressing us. He gives us a choice to believe the lie or trade it for truth. I'd like to say this was easy, but it's not. It's simple, not easy, but so worth the process. And to be honest, our old habits or pathways often feel normal, familiar, or comfortable. We have created such deep brain pathways over the years that it has taken and will take many intentional steps to retrain our thinking and beliefs. This won't be done with self-effort or on our own but only with the leading of a loving God and godly counsel. It's also an ongoing process of learning and becoming more of who God created us to be.

I've struggled with knowing and living in my identity in Christ, and I've also been set free. It's a one-time deliverance and a process all at the same time. I need to continue to remind myself and work it out . . . keep my eyes fixed on Jesus and continually seek Him and grow and learn. I am free, and you can be, too.

So, when I saw the truth, I had a choice. I could see the names and labels the world and people had given me. I could see the labels and judgments I'd held over myself, and I could see the words and identity God has for me. Which one do I want? What will I focus on? What am I basing my beliefs and faith in?

It's ultimately our choice to continue living in the same patterns that got us here or to take God's word for it. My basketball coach always used to say, "If you do what you've always done, you'll get what you've always gotten." This is true in all areas of life; your life won't change unless you decide you will change. Yes, you might still hear those voices in your mind or in the world, but you can also see and hear the truth. Do you want people, jobs, or the world to hold your value? Do you want to work, earn, and please to gain acceptance and status? Or do you want the free gift of God's loving words over you? Which will you grab hold of? Which will you cling to? The choice is ultimately yours because God is so gracious, and He gives us free will.

I decided, "As for me and my house, we will serve the LORD" (Joshua 24:15, NIV). That is what we will set our minds to, our hearts to, and our identities to. When you get to a place where you see you have the choice, you will come to the end of being victim to all that's around you, and "the truth will set you free" (John 8:32, NIV). Then, "If the Son sets you free, you will be free indeed" (John 8:36, NIV).

After many hours of counseling and spiritual mentoring, I could see my old thoughts, patterns, and behaviors for what they were—lies—and I could finally see the truth. The lies held me captive for so long that I desired to be free. The beliefs and old ways of processing and thinking didn't serve me anymore. They cost me enough. I came to the place where I needed to renew my mind; God needed to renew my mind. I needed to replace the lies with the truth of the Word of God and continually remind myself, my soul, of who I am. I did this daily, even sometimes hourly, until I believed the truth of what God says about me to my core; even now, it's continual growth and practice I do daily.

Earlier on in my journey, I would write affirmations to remind myself who I was in Christ. My brother encouraged me to keep a record, to write down who I was daily. It was not enough to just read it. To really make it stick, I needed to read it, write it, and speak it. It needed to become a part of me, deeply engrained in my belief. In short, he was telling me to do this to create new brain pathways. What we focus on is what we become; what we focus on is what we move towards. I wanted to move towards truth and not the lies, fears, or past experiences that I had encountered.

I found it helpful to take the lies I believed that I felt like the world, circumstances, or my own insecurities said about me and search for what the Word of God said about me instead. I then formed affirmations to say over myself each morning and each night. I posted them in my bathroom and began to speak the affirmations aloud. I also wrote them in journals, on note cards in my purse, or on a note on my phone. I had the truth of who I was readily available whenever I had a thought or memory contradictory to God's Word. If I was grocery shopping and started to have negative thoughts, I'd pull out my note cards and read affirmations over myself as I walked the aisles. While I was driving, I'd listen to worship music, pray, or speak out loud over and over, "I am loved. I am safe. I am enough." I equipped myself so that wherever I was when those memories or thoughts hit, I was prepared. In essence, I began changing the neural pathways in my brain.

Picture the neural pathways (ways of thinking) in your brain as trails in the woods. Every time you have a thought, it's like walking the same path through the woods. The more you walk the same path, the more worn the trail gets. The grass soon disappears, and a dirt trail is formed. The more foot traffic it has, the wider and more obvious the trail becomes. Pretty soon, the trail that you have made seems to be the only way clear through the forest. There are other ways to move through the woods, but the mind takes the path of least resistance, so it seems that the only natural option is that dirt trail.

It's much like driving to a familiar place. The first time you drive to a new job, you might use directions, look at the road signs, and really pay attention to the landmarks in the area. The next day of work, you might not need directions, but you are aware of the roads and specific turns you need to make. After a while, driving to work becomes automatic. You don't need to think about the path, the roads, or landmarks. Your mind and body know what to do. You might even get in your car, sip your coffee while contemplating an important conversation you just had with a friend, and wind up in the parking lot at work not remembering how you actually drove there. (Purely an example . . . of course.) Your mind is amazing. It works this way, and it can be very helpful for things like tying your shoes, riding a bike, or typing on a computer, but it can also be very dangerous if you don't know what you are automated in.

Think about what you are thinking about. Observe the way you participate in relationships. Check your motives. Notice the things you say to yourself, and assess whether you want these thoughts, patterns, and behaviors in your life. Are they hurting you or helping you? It's time to get rid of the lies, false beliefs, and harmful patterns, so you can actually hold the truth. You can't change what you aren't first aware of. This is challenging. It takes courage, strength, and humility to look at yourself and admit your need to change. Remember to look at yourself through the lens of grace. God is allowing you to see what's holding you back. He isn't judging you for it; it's His love that is helping expose the pain and hurt to bring healing and wholeness.

Digging into the Word of God and finding what God says about me, my identity, and my truth really set me free. It allowed me to see who I really am . . . to assess how I participate in relationships and why I act the way I do. The truth set me free from the cycle of pleasing and working for my value because I could see I was already loved by God. Already chosen, forgiven, and enough in Christ. Finding my truest identity in God set me free from codependency, fear, false expectations, and reacting to the world around me. It set me free from basing my identity on success, failure, circumstance, and other people's opinions. Finding my identity in Christ gave me true freedom.

I'm going to challenge you to do the same. Think about the things in your mind that have been replaying or the words that have been spoken over you. Stop and think about the words you speak to yourself that are limiting you: *I'm not enough. I'm a failure. I'll never be able to. . . . I don't deserve love. I don't deserve forgiveness.*

Write these lies, hurtful words, or limiting statements down. Get them out, identify them, and face your fears. We can't heal and change without first addressing our issues, patterns, and lies. Sometimes we think that looking at the fears will break us, make the lie stronger, or even create more toxicity. The opposite is true. Addressing our fears, lies, and misconceptions helps us take back our authority and power. It disarms the lie. It allows us to see the root of the issue, heal, move through the pain, and get stronger. Facing our fears empowers us. We know what they are anyway; let's stop them from hanging out in the back of our minds and tormenting us. Let's pull them forward and out, so we can debunk the lies and instill the truth.

Limiting Statements, Lies, and False Beliefs

When we take out the bad, we need to fill those spaces in our hearts and minds with good. We don't want to leave ourselves empty. Let's start by praying over the lies and asking the Holy Spirit to cleanse us and help us be filled with truth. Here is an example of a short prayer:

Father,

Thank You for loving me so much and showing me the lies and patterns that are holding me back. Forgive me for participating in and believing these lies about myself. I give these lies to You. I ask You to wash my mind, body, and spirit of all effects and memories of these patterns and lies with the blood of Jesus. Now Jesus, will You come and fill me with Your love, peace, and truth? Speak to me the words You say about me. Tell me who You say that I am. I want to renew my mind and my identity in You. Thank You, Jesus. Amen

Truth and Affirmation

It takes courage and strength to look at yourself, show yourself grace, and begin to grow. Now that you have acknowledged the lies and false beliefs and you have "gotten rid of them," it's time for you to choose the truth and create new ways of thinking and new patterns for your mind. For me, that was by creating affirmations to train my mind and remind myself of the truth.

I started by looking up Bible verses that showed me what truth is—opposite the lies: I am enough in Christ. I am chosen, loved, and forgiven. I am God's child who was made in the image of Christ. The first step to your new identity is knowing what the Bible says about you, knowing how God fashioned you and gifted you. Remember, when God sees you, He sees Jesus. Your new identity is Jesus. You are now a co-heir with Christ. You are a child of God. Below I'll walk you through a short process for finding truth and writing an affirmation.

Let's get to work. Let's start together to develop an affirmation for you. It could be a sentence, a paragraph, or a whole list of things. Write out who you are. Dig into Scripture for yourself. Write what you discover in a journal or on the mirror in your bathroom. Plaster your office or home with note-cards or Post-its. Write and post the truth in the visual spaces where you live and work. Set reminders on your phone to tell you who you are every hour or every ten minutes if you need that. Remind your soul, spirit, and body of who you are. God gave you a voice to speak. He gave you the authority to speak out the truth over yourself—so do it!

Below are some affirmations and declarations that I have written over myself. I also put the affirmation I have my children speak over themselves each night before they go to bed. Just as important as it is to remind yourself of who you are, if you are a parent, grandparent, or mentor, it's your job and honor to teach your kids who God says they are. Make this the legacy you pass on.

An affirmation can be as involved or simple as you want it to be. Start with prayer and ask God's Holy Spirit in you to lead you to what His words are regarding you. Your affirmation might change in different seasons to focus on specific areas, but it will always be the Word of God. It will always be His truth, and it will always be His love.

In different seasons, mine have evolved. I started with a list of three things.

1) I am loved.

2) I am chosen.

3) I am enough.

Those evolved into an entire list of affirmations with Bible verses.

» I am loved. (Ephesians 2:4-5)

» I am a new creation. (2 Corinthians 5:17)

» I am a child of God. (1 John 3:1)

» I am forgiven. (Ephesians 1:7)

» I have the mind of Christ. (1 Corinthians 2:16)

» I am chosen. (Ephesians 1:4-5 and Peter 2:9)

» God's grace is lavished on me. (Ephesians 1:7-9)

» I am blessed with every spiritual blessing in Christ. (Ephesians 1:3)

» The Spirit of God (Holy Spirit) lives in me. (1 John 4:4 and Ephesians 1:13-14)

» I am holy and blameless in His sight . . . made righteous by Christ. (Ephesians 1:4-5)

» I am a daughter of the King . . . adopted and accepted. (1 John 1:12, 1 John 3:1, and 2 Corinthians 8:18)

> » I am complete in Christ. (Colossians 2:9-10)
> » I have the peace of God that surpasses all understanding. (Philippians 4:7)

I am love, joy, peace, patience, kindness, goodness, faithfulness, and self-control. I am light. I am loved. I am a child of the King. I am who God says I am. (My children's affirmation)

In no way is this a complete list of who God says we are, but it's a start. Use it to set you on your own journey of discovering who God made you to be. The searching and seeking for yourself is where truth seeps deep into your soul, and you see and believe it for yourself.

Now, these words and this identity, they are love. They are a love that no human, job, position, or possession can offer. His love is a sure thing . . . a relationship to trust . . . a love that fills my soul, never runs dry, expires, or runs out. The best part is that it's free. Yes, free. A gift, given by God, to us. Not dependent on me or my behavior; it is 100 percent based on Jesus and His love for me.

What love can compare to this? You are loved, chosen, saved, forgiven, made new, strong, and highly valued. These are promises to stand on and truth you should let sink into your heart. God loves you, and nothing can separate you from the love of God according to Romans 8:35, 37-39 (ESV):

> *Who shall separate us from the love of Christ? Shall tribulation, or distress, or persecution, or famine, or nakedness, or danger, or sword. . . .*
>
> *No, in all these things we are more than conquerors through him who loved us. For I am sure that neither death nor life, nor angels nor rulers, nor things present nor things to come, nor powers, nor height nor depth, nor anything else in all creation,*

will be able to separate us from the love of God in Christ Jesus
our Lord.

It was brought to my attention that this verse doesn't say anything
about the past. It mentions the present and future and covers all other
aspects of life yet not the past. I started to wonder and have conversations about this verse and what it could possibly mean. Could it be
possible that without healing the lies and past wounds of our lives we
are hindered from deeper intimacy with God and others?

I believe that the love of God is greater than everything (even the
past), yet I have also experienced that the lies I believed regarding my
past experiences held me back from the love that God was offering.
It wasn't that the past stopped God's love; it didn't. God's love was
always there, but the past did block me from seeing and receiving
what was always right in front of me. It was through breaking down
these strongholds in my mind and heart that I was truly able to experience the love of God, see it more clearly, and accept it.

As I began to process the past, I began to see the faithfulness of
God interwoven in all my experiences. God's love and forgiveness
covered them all. The past is no longer; it exists only as a memory.
God's love, grace, and mercy cover it all. Yet I believe that the enemy
uses our past as bait and ammunition against us. The enemy would
love it if we felt guilt and shame over the past, held on to unforgiveness, and were blinded to grace and love. There is nothing new under
the sun. This is the enemy's MO: shame, blame, and taunting you
with unforgiveness and past failures. The enemy can't stop God's
love and mercy from covering the past, present, or future, so his goal
is to distract us and get us to believe the lie that our past can keep
us from God when the reality is that grace is the foundation of our
faith. Forgiveness through Jesus is the gateway to freedom allowing

access to the love of the Father. The past can't stop or separate us from God's love, but it can restrict us from seeing the love that is available to us.

||||||||||||||||||||||||||||||||||||||||||||||||||||||||||||||||||||||||||||||||||||||||||||

The past can't stop or separate us from God's love, but it can restrict us from seeing the love that is available to us.

||||||||||||||||||||||||||||||||||||||||||||||||||||||||||||||||||||||||||||||||||||||||||||

Now it's your turn. Use this book as a workbook. Ask God to highlight the lies you have believed about yourself, others, and even God. Use the list you created on the previous page as the Holy Spirit leads you; see the lie, write it down, and then find God's truth. If you are struggling with value, search online Bible verses on God's love. If you are struggling with depression, search Bible verses on joy and hope. Often, it's hard to just open the Bible and know where to start. Don't get overwhelmed. Start small, and use the tools you have.

Once you've found a verse that speaks the truth to your life, and you've written it down, read it, speak it out loud, and study it. After you have sat with this verse, create a personal affirmation using your name or "I," and then speak it to yourself. You get to choose what you say; really, the only thing you can control in life is your choices. So, choose life! Choose to speak God's truth and love. If there is something that needs healing, be real with yourself and God. Allow God to show you the truth. Seek counsel, and do the hard work. God is with you, and He will guide you to all truth through the Holy Spirit.

Here are a couple of examples of the affirmations I have for myself:

Lie/False Belief:

I am not enough; I don't have value or worth.

Truth/Bible Verses:

"For all have sinned and fall short of the glory of God and are justified by his grace as a gift." (Romans 3:23, ESV)

"For God so loved the world that he gave his one and only son that whoever believes in him shall not perish but have everlasting life." (John 3:16, NIV)

"For we are God's masterpiece. He has created us anew in Christ Jesus, so we can do the good things he planned for us long ago." (Ephesians 2:10, NLT)

Affirmation:

I am not perfect, but God does not expect that from me. I am saved and justified by the blood of Jesus. God wanted me and saved me by paying with His Son. I am of great worth to God. He loves me. He also made me: mind, body, and spirit. I am a masterpiece . . . a divine creation. I was made as I am. I am enough—created on purpose by God.

Lie/False Belief:

I can't like myself or think positively about myself.

Truth/Bible Verse:

"'Love your neighbor as yourself.' There is no commandment greater. . . ." (Mark 12:31, NIV)

Affirmation:

God made me. He created me. To not love and respect myself would go against God. I think, believe, and speak positively about myself. He said I should love my neighbor as myself. To the degree I love myself, I'm able to love, serve, and give grace to others.

In the statements above, you were able to see the truth of who you are. Use the contents of this book and the verses you find in Scripture, and see what God says about you and the areas you struggle with. God is so cool. He has led me on such a personal journey with Him; He is an intimate God, He is close, and He cares. He cares even about the small details of your life. Seek Him; you won't be disappointed. It's your turn. Use the template below to address the lies and false beliefs you are struggling with and work on your affirmations.

Lie/False Belief:

_____

_____

_____

_____

Truth/Bible Verse:

_____

_____

_____

_____

Affirmation:

_____

_____

_____

_____

Lie/False Belief:

_____

_____

_____

_____

Truth/Bible Verse:

_____

_____

_____

_____

Affirmation:

_____

_____

_____

_____

Lie/False Belief:

_____

_____

_____

_____

Truth/Bible Verse:

_____

_____

_____

_____

Affirmation:

_____

_____

_____

_____

After you go through this process, recognize the lies you've believed, and find the truth, I believe it's important to drop the lie. Ask the Holy Spirit what He'd have you do with the lie. Maybe you can color the lie in red marker, showing it's covered by the blood of Jesus. Maybe you can cut the lie off the page and throw it away, burn it, or wash it in water. The important piece for me was taking the lie and letting it go—showing myself and the enemy that this lie, or false belief, no longer has power over me. It's a liberating and freeing experience to choose in life. Over time, as I continue to say the affirmations I have created, I don't even remember the lies that used to be attached. My mind is being healed. Friend, I hope you see freedom.

SCENE TWO

CHAPTER 8

Teatime

God wants you to spill the tea. While that saying refers to gossip, I'm trying to say that God wants to know what's on your heart. He also wants you to know what's on His heart. God is a personal God. He desires to bring you healing and set you free. He also desires a friendship and relationship with you. He wants to spend time with you, talk to you, meet with you, and sit with you.

Isn't that what our deepest desire is too? To know and be known? Our heart's desire is intimacy, and that's God's too. That God desires to build a relationship with you might be a new concept; it might even seem a little odd. How can you have a relationship with an invisible God?

There's no right or wrong way to do this; relationships are all different because we are all different. We connect through different ways and experiences. Think about your life: When do you feel God's presence? When do you hear God speak? How do you make space to hear from God? Maybe you're thinking, *How do I even do that? Is that possible?* The answer is yes.

The Bible

God is always with you. Often, we humans are unaware of His active presence in our lives. Our lives are so full of responsibilities and noise that we don't pause long enough to see, notice, and hear Him. People hear from God in many ways: through music, books, nature, writing, and praying. God can really speak through anything. The most common and easily seen is through His written Word, the Bible. 2 Timothy 3:16-17 (BSB) explains it this way:

All scripture is God-breathed and is useful for instruction, for conviction, for correction, and for training in righteousness, so that the man of God may be complete, fully equipped for every good work. . . .

The Bible is more than a list of rules to follow. It's meant to help us by sharing God's love with us. Timothy says that God gave us this book to train us, instruct us, and equip us. We are to use this book as a manual to be complete. The Bible is God's personal love story to us; it's the love story of the ages and God's spoken words to us. It beats any Hallmark, Disney, or romantic comedy that we've seen. The reason it's better is that it's real.

||||||||||||||||||||||||||||||||||||||||||||||||||||||||||||||||||||||||||||||||||||||||||||||||||||||

The Bible is God's personal love story to us; it's the love story of the ages and God's spoken words to us.

||||||||||||||||||||||||||||||||||||||||||||||||||||||||||||||||||||||||||||||||||||||||||||||||||||||

The Bible doesn't end at "happily ever after." It does *have* a happily ever after—our life with God in eternity—but it also has help, guidance, freedom, and grace for the here and now. You don't have to wait until the end of your life to experience the happily ever after. God wants to give it to you now: in the middle of the mess, the loss, and the in-between. God is here now with hope, joy, and freedom. God wants to have a relationship with you. He is with you . . . available to you. He desires to know you and for you to know Him.

Throughout the Bible, we see God's faithfulness, love, and grace woven through the lives and stories shared. There are accounts of hundreds of people who had encounters with God; you see the birth of Jesus and hear of His healing and teaching. There is instruction, or boundaries, that lead to a life of freedom and security. There are songs of praise and phrases of wisdom that are meant to guide and build your faith. The Bible shows God's faithfulness through generations of Israelite people. It shows how His grace is given to the Gentiles (non-Jews) through Jesus. God used people like Rehab, who was a prostitute, and Ruth, who was a Moabite and a foreigner, to bring about His redemption through Jesus. All of this because He loved us.

Hebrews 4:12 (AMP) says the Bible is the living Word of God:

> For the word of God is living and active and full of power [making it operative, energizing, and effective]. It is sharper than any two-edged-sword, penetrating as far as the division of the soul and spirit [the completeness of a person], and of both joints and marrow [the deepest parts of our nature], exposing and judging the very thoughts and intentions of the heart.

We read the Bible, but the Bible also "reads" us. Certain words and phrases jump out at us. The words can highlight areas of our lives that we are hiding or didn't even know were there. The words can also bring healing and comfort. I was reading in the book of Isaiah one day—a passage I'd read multiple times before—but this day it landed differently. I felt like God was speaking directly to me:

"Fear not, for you will not be ashamed;
be not confounded, for you will not be disgraced;
for you will forget the shame of your youth,
and the reproach of your widowhood you will remember no more.
For your Maker is your husband,
the LORD of hosts is his name;
and the Holy One of Israel is your Redeemer,
the God of the whole earth he is called. . . .
"For the mountains may depart
and the hills be removed,
but my steadfast love shall not depart from you,
and my covenant of peace shall not be removed,"
says the LORD, who has compassion on you.
—Isaiah 54:4-5, 10 (ESV)

The words of this scripture brought a deep-seated peace. It settled my core, and I felt loved. It was written so long ago, but at that moment, those verses came alive to me. It was a promise that God was with me; He was my redeemer, my husband. His love would never leave me, and His peace would never leave me. In a season where my life was flipped upside down, this was the firm foundation that I needed. This is what my heart was desiring: someone to lean on . . . secure and sure. This was a new experience for me, to have a physical feeling deep in my heart. It was as if God were right in front of me, speaking out loud of His love and promise to be with me.

If you are wondering if you can hear from God, the answer is yes. Start by praying and asking the Holy Spirit to speak to you and reveal what He wants you to see through the scripture you are reading. Start reading your Bible. The New Testament is a great place to start, but also check out Psalms and Proverbs. Read through the verses and underline words or phrases that pop out at you. Then listen. Write down what you sense and observe, what you think the verse is saying, and what that would mean for your life. My church likes to call this process SOAP: Scripture, Observation (what I notice), Application (how it pertains to my life), and Prayer. It's an easy format to keep track of what you are learning and reading.

Other Ways to Hear God

There are many ways to hear God. I've experienced God speaking to me through pictures in my mind, understanding (something I just sense and know in my spirit), or speaking to me through mentors, movies, novels, nonfiction texts, nature, or my kids. Think about how you hear or feel the presence of God. He is constantly with us; He promises to never leave us or forsake us (Deuteronomy 31:8). Usually, our awareness or lack of awareness of God keeps us from seeing and hearing Him. Remember, God's desire is for intimacy with you, connection, and relationship.

It took me a while to figure out how to become aware of God's voice. Sometimes I feel internal "gut" promptings. That is the Holy Spirit alerting me in the moment. I've felt God speak to me through song lyrics, movie scenes, and even book characters. God can use anything to teach you and help you see the truth. God can speak to you through thought. An idea pops into my head at the store or in a conversation with my children that is exactly what I need at that moment.

Often, we mislabel the voice of God as intuition, coincidence, or our own brilliance. God is not limited to speaking a certain way. I find that He speaks to me in one way for a time and then appears to shift to revealing Himself in another way. I often wonder if He isn't revealing Himself always, and it's just my awareness and recognition that changes.

I began seeing God in places and ways I had not experienced before. This continues to keep my heart seeking God and not get caught in the means in which He speaks or limit Him to my ideas and experience.

For the last few years, I have heard God through writing. I pour out everything I'm thinking into a journal as a letter to God. After I get my thoughts out, I have more space in my mind and spirit to hear Him. I write down my questions or frustrations, and then I sit and listen for God to respond. At first, I was skeptical, as you might be, but He speaks and responds to me like a conversation. It comes across as thoughts in my mind in response to what I've written. Sometimes, the response comes even before I finish writing the question! I log God's response in my journal as well as my own. It often looks like a conversation in a novel, a dialogue between two people, and that's precisely what it is.

When I started this practice of prayer or conversation with God each night at teatime, I was hesitant. I didn't want to "hear wrong" or make up things in my head. I had many conversations with my spiritual mentor about how to recognize when God is speaking to me, and here is a quick checklist. God speaks what is consistent with His character: love, truth, and life.

» Is it the truth? (Does it line up with the Bible? Does it speak life?)
» Is it consistent with God's character? (Is it a fruit of the Spirit? Is it love?)
» Correction or condemnation? (Is it filled with grace and hope . . . or shame?)
» Am I yielded or controlling? (Am I open to hearing God or trying to control outcomes?)

The important thing to notice when you are listening is what voice you are listening to: The Holy Spirit, the devil, yourself? It's good to check the things we hear. Is what you heard or what was impressed on you in line with the Word of God? If not, it's not from God. Does it reflect the character of God? Is it spoken with kindness, love, and truth? Does it reflect the fruit of the Spirit: love, joy, peace, patience, kindness, goodness, faithfulness, and self-control? Is what you are hearing meant to control or manipulate you? If so, then it's not from God. Check what you are hearing. Remember that God is love, and through His love, He also corrects, heals, and points out places for growth. It's never through condemnation or judgment—that's the enemy. It's always covered in love.

God is a God of order. He is a God of truth, of love, and of comfort. That means that God will correct you, but His correction does not have condemnation; according to Romans 8:1 (NIV), "There is no condemnation for those who are in Christ Jesus." I've heard and experienced that God usually disciplines or corrects you with a "love sandwich." God will show you His love, kindly correct you, heal you, and then show His love again. He is a good and kind Father; His correction heals and builds.

God also prunes; He cuts off the things and cuts out the places in your life that are holding you back. This feels hard, but to be able to grow real fruit, a tree needs pruning, and so do we. We have many thoughts, behaviors, and ways of living that aren't in line with the truth. Pruning doesn't feel good. I don't like the process of cutting out things in my life that feel comfortable or that have been with me for many years. Comfort can become the opposite of growth. It doesn't mean that it is healthy or good for you. Comfort just means you are used to it. You can be comfortable with abuse, poor self-talk, or codependency. I'm not saying you like any of these things, but they feel normal; we've learned to tolerate them. Sometimes, we'd rather stay with what we know than risk the unknown. The unknown is not comfortable. It's risky, but staying comfortable can keep you trapped.

Another way I have experienced hearing God is through a prayer ministry and prayer time with my counselor. Several people have helped me pray and invite the Holy Spirit into the hurt areas of my life to release His healing and love. Through these opportunities, I have let go of unforgiveness, control, pride, judgment, doubt, and fear. As I have prayed and released my heart to the healing work of the Holy Spirit, He has enabled my ability to see and hear. It's as if my eyes and ears have been opened, and I can see and hear more clearly. It feels as if the white noise of life is gone; my heart and mind have stilled, and I can hear in the silence.

I have experienced God giving me pictures and images in my head and showing me how much He loves me. These pictures or visions have brought healing, truth, and hope to me on my journey. Inviting the Holy Spirit into your pain and hurt allows Him to do the work in you. I have experienced a deeper level of spiritual, emotional, and physical healing as I've walked through prayer ministry.

God desires to speak to you, and yes, it's possible, through the Holy Spirit, to hear Him. Set aside some time to just sit, wherever you feel comfortable, and listen. Turn off all distractions, get all the thoughts and demands of life out of your head, and allow yourself to be in the present moment. This takes practice and time, but as you practice presence and hearing the voice of God, it will become like riding a bike, easier and easier to do, and one day it will become like second nature. This is the space where your body, soul, and spirit are present and aware of hearing God speak.

Teatime

One night I was sitting in my bed having tea; I was sick and wanted something warm to drink. In this moment of silence, I asked God to speak to me. I was tired and exhausted from being sick and parenting solo; I felt like I had nothing left. In that space of need, I heard (through my thoughts) God say, *Will you have tea with me every night?* The funny thing is that I don't even like tea. But I know it's not about the tea; it's about the time.

I took that as an invitation, and I began setting that time aside each night to have tea with Jesus. Each night after I put my children to bed, I make tea and sit on my bed. As I close my eyes and pray, I visualize Jesus sitting with me on the end of the bed drinking His tea. That time, I started talking to Him as I would talk to a friend I went out for coffee with. I was in a deep season of change and loneliness, and I felt the Holy Spirit prompting me to allow Him to fill those places in my life where relationships had changed, and I felt loss and lack. At first, it felt odd and even silly, but as I continued each night to pour out my heart and questions, God showed up.

Really, God was there with me all along; it's more like I showed up with open ears, a quiet mind, and a desire to hear. (Isn't that what we all long for and want in a relationship? Someone to show up, to listen, to care, and to love us?) Some nights, I felt as though God were speaking to me with pictures in my mind of my kids and me, ways in which God was with us through the hard season we were walking. Other nights, I heard His words over me—His promises to me—very clearly in thoughts in my mind. It flowed like a conversation full of truth and love. And some nights, I sat in silent peace, feeling His presence and sensing His love.

God met me there whether I entered the time eager, tired, expectant, or reluctant. He met me with love, patience, truth, and respect. He didn't push when I wasn't open, but He still stayed. He will always stay with me; He will stay with you too.

God delights in you. I want you to see, feel, and understand that. Too often in life, I have felt like I'm a burden or more of someone to tolerate. I'm not sure why I've felt that way. Honestly, I have a truly loving family and friends, but that lie has been hidden deep in my mind and heart. I've used that perspective to view many of my experiences in life, and I started to view God that way. That I am a burden to Him is very clearly a lie. Through my experience of having tea with God each night, He has communicated to me that His feelings are the opposite.

Zephaniah 3:17 (NIV) says, "The LORD your God is with you, the Mighty Warrior who saves. He will take great delight in you; in his love, he will no longer rebuke you, but will rejoice over you with singing." This verse has shifted my perspective on how I view God and His love for me. It has been a comfort to me on lonely nights and days when I feel unseen or less than. This truth resets my perspective and helps me see God as my warrior and loving Savior. It's a picture of the perfect love that I desire—presence, protection, care, love, delight, and joy.

Having teatime each night has been so cool. I've seen God's love for me, forgiveness, and care. I've felt His humor, light-heartedness, and patience. It felt like a true friendship blossoming, and it was new for me. God is present, God is good, and God is faithful. He is with us whether we see Him or not. Some days we just "feel" alone or stuck. These are days that I must remind my soul and preach to myself the truth. Psalm 103 (NIV) describes it:

Praise the LORD, my soul;
all my inmost being, praise his holy name.
Praise the LORD, my soul,
and forget not all his benefits—
who forgives all your sins
and heals all your diseases,

who redeems your life from the pit
and crowns you with love and compassion,
who satisfies your desires with good things
so that your youth is renewed like the eagles.

This is the truth, and on hard days and good days, I am learning to remind myself of it and speak it to my spirit. Although I may feel sad, alone, or lonely, this is the truth: God is with me. God is for me. And God is good.

We all know that having coffee (or tea) together or going out to lunch is not about the actual food that we eat but the time that we spend together. The quality time spent sharing our hearts, our stories, and our love with each other is what bonds us in relationships; this is connection. That's what God wants with you. Yes, you might be thinking, *He's not physically in front of me; I can't see or hear an audible voice.* I get that; I've struggled with that too, but God is more real than the reality of the physical thing sitting in front of you. Just because you can't see God doesn't mean you can't feel Him, hear Him, or see His hand on your life.

|||||||||||||||||||||||||||||||||||||||||||||||||||||||||||||||||||||||||||||||||||||||||||||||||||

> Just because you can't see God doesn't mean you can't feel Him, hear Him, or see His hand on your life.

|||||||||||||||||||||||||||||||||||||||||||||||||||||||||||||||||||||||||||||||||||||||||||||||||||

It's like the sun; you know it's in the sky. You can see it and feel its warmth, but you don't panic and fret on a cloudy day because you can't see it. You know it's still there. Clouds might cover it, but you can still feel its warmth and the effects of the light brightening the sky even through the clouds. Plants continue to grow, even on cloudy days, and if you are fair-skinned like me, you can even get a sunburn through the clouds. Just because you can't see something doesn't mean it's not powerful and present in your life.

So, I challenge you to shift your focus or keep your focus on awareness of God. Start to see Him in your daily life; He is everywhere. Even the breath you are breathing is from Him. The reality that your heart continues to beat, and your brain can read this information is proof of your Creator. Close your eyes, picture Jesus sitting across from you, and talk to Him like He's your friend. Join me in having tea with Jesus. If tea isn't your thing, then run with Jesus, lift weights with Jesus, paint, draw . . . you get the picture.

» Listen to a worship song.

» Go for a run/walk outdoors.

» Be creative—paint, draw, build, etc.

» Sit in silence.

» Focus on gratitude.

» Write in a journal.

If you don't know where to start when talking to God, simply thank Him for the things that you have in your life. Thank Him for His presence, and thank Him for His love. If you are like me, you might have a thousand questions for God. Ask the questions! Even if you don't get an answer to a specific question, God is faithful to respond and speak life to you. Many times, when I ask a specific question, instead of an answer, God asks me to trust Him or reminds me of His love for me. Don't let unanswered questions stop you. Here are some open-ended questions to get you started:

» Ask God what is on His heart.

» Ask God what He wants to show you or teach you.

» Ask God whom He wants you to connect with, pray for, serve, or help.

» Ask God His perspective on your situation or life.

» Ask God how He sees you.

And then listen. Quiet the noise. Silence your phone. Still your mind and heart. Make space in your schedule to listen and hear. Be present and aware in the current moment you are in. The other amazing thing about spending time with God is that you are often left with peace and joy. Psalm 16:11 (ESV) says: "You make known to me the path of life; in your presence, there is fullness of joy; at your right hand are pleasures forevermore." Although God is the God of the past, present, and future, He wants you to live in the present moment. He is there with you, and in His presence, there is fullness of joy.

The main idea I want you to get from this chapter is that God desires to spend time with you in relationship. God wants to know your heart and for you to know His. He desires to speak to you; He desires intimacy and connection. There are many ways to hear from God; He always reveals Himself and speaks. "You will seek me and find me, when you seek me with all your heart" (Jeremiah 29:13, ESV).

CHAPTER 9

My Safe Haven

*I*f real life followed the scripts and scenes of the movies, it would be predictable and steady. There would be some excitement, maybe a little trouble (not too much), but it would always be resolved quickly, and all the drama would be nicely tied in a bow by the end of the movie. If you have watched many rom-coms or Hallmark movies, you see the fallacy in what is presented . . . life starts with the happily ever after, not ends. The drama is light, even funny, and the pain that is experienced is enough to pull at your heartstrings yet still give you hope for a good ending. The movies we love always end with " . . . and they lived happily ever after." They don't continue; they can't. If they continued, we'd see that life is still life, people fall short, relationships end, and pain and suffering happen. Life isn't as predictable and steady as we'd like. If it were, it wouldn't require faith.

We write scripts that end in joy, peace, and love all based on positive circumstances in the characters' lives. But what happens when it doesn't work out the way you planned . . . you don't get the job . . . the relationship doesn't work out . . . you are hurt and wounded, and it was not your fault? What if money is still tight, and you can't catch a break? What happens when the credits of our lives roll, and the pain is still there?

If I'm honest, I'd love it if following Jesus meant no pain, trouble, or hardship. Security to me has meant happy, positive circumstances and relationships. And if I'm being *really* honest, I held this view for most of my life. I thought that if God were with me, and I did all the right things (hello, self-righteousness), then nothing truly terrible could ever happen to me. Yep. That's right. You called it: wrong belief. Not reality, not the truth, and found nowhere in the Bible. Yes, I do live on earth—that place where there is that thing called sin.

||||||||||||||||||||||||||||||||||||||||||||||||||||||||||||||||||||||||||||||||||||||||||||||||||||||||||||||

> ### Security is knowing that no matter what happens to me in life, this is still true: God loves me, God is with me, God will help me, and God will heal me.

||||||||||||||||||||||||||||||||||||||||||||||||||||||||||||||||||||||||||||||||||||||||||||||||||||||||||||||

So, reality came in like a hurricane when my life was turned upside down with betrayal, deception, and divorce. With an incorrect belief system based on what we discussed above, my view about God, life, and myself was turned upside down. To spare you the details, here is what I found to be true: we live in a broken world, sin is present, and people are imperfect. But I also found this to be true: God is still faithful, God is with me and never leaves me, and God redeems brokenness.

Security is not found in perfect circumstances (although I continue to desire this) but in a relationship with Jesus. Security is knowing that no matter what happens to me in life, this is still true: God loves me,

God is with me, God will help me, and God will heal me. In Romans 8:28 (NIV), it says, "And we know that in all things God works for the good of those who love him, who have been called according to his purpose."

God will provide for me and works on my behalf. God is a good God. His plans for me are good. His plans for you are good. Life is not always good, and more often than we'd like, we experience circumstances that cause trouble and pain. Sometimes they are caused by us, and sometimes things happen to us. Either way, God takes all things and works them out for our good. Now, hear me. Not all things are good. Life can be hard, and pain is real. I have experience with this, and I have struggled at times to see the good. In the middle of the pit—the problem—it's hard to see this truth. I've been there and said, "Nothing good can come from this." I've thought to myself, *Surely my life is ruined, and now I'm left with a subpar life that will never be what I'd hoped.*

If you are there, I see you. I value your experience and pain, and I'm so sorry for what you have had to walk through. It's not fair. I also know it is hard to see the light when you are sifting through all the dirt and mud. Feeling hopelessness and despair is real; feel it, but please don't stay there. Yes, there is a time to grieve; that is a very important process in healing. Seek a counselor, seek help, and walk through your emotions. I've done the work and continue to do my personal healing work as I travel through this life. It is important.

I also want you to hear this: there is always hope. Don't sit, pitch a tent, or stay in the pit. That is a dangerous place to live, and so many of us stop there because we can't see the way out. I'm here to help you stand up and dust yourself off. I'll walk out with you hand in hand. You can't see the light? Neither could I, but I started walking, and you can too. I'm here to say there is hope. It isn't hope for perfect circumstances or to take away what has happened to you. It is hope for you—the person inside who is desperate to be saved, to be rescued, and to be loved.

You might not see it now, but take my word for it. God is faithful. He has taken my life's broken, messy muck and mud, and turned it all for good. He can also work all the hard and broken places in your life for good as well. Hear me; it still hurt. It still cost me a lot. I had to grieve and feel all the feels, but in that honest and broken place, God came and brought beauty. He brought a new perspective, comfort, truth, and love.

||||||||||||||||||||||||||||||||||||||||||||||||||||||||||||||||||||||||||||||||||||||||||||

God is faithful. He has taken my life's broken, messy muck and mud, and turned it all for good.

||||||||||||||||||||||||||||||||||||||||||||||||||||||||||||||||||||||||||||||||||||||||||||

I remember thinking one day early in my journey, *I will never be the person who says, "I wish I wouldn't have gone through it, but I am so thankful for what I've learned."* Honestly, people said that to me, and I was frustrated with it. It felt like they didn't value me, my pain, or my loss. (I do understand it now and believe it. But hear me: I'm not saying that to you.) I am saying that there is hope, not just to be patched back together, barely hanging on, but to be made stronger, more beautiful, and more alive than you have ever been. There is hope to be made whole.

Because God is God, He can take what the enemy (or our own sin) meant for evil and turn it for good. It means that whatever comes, good or bad (or neutral), passes through God's hands. He promises to be with us through it, to work good from it, and grow us in it.

That deep floundering in my soul—the unsettling feeling in people, circumstances, and systems—was driving me to find something or someone to land on. And that is Jesus. Jesus is secure. I can cling to Him; He is my haven. He is pure, safe, and outside of change, time, and unstable people and circumstances.

If you find yourself in a season of insecurity, remind yourself that no matter what happens in your life, God is with you, and He will help you through it. He will never leave you, and He will work it all out for your good, according to His purpose for you. What is the truth you need to tell yourself in this season of disappointment and uneasiness?

Read Psalm 23 (ESV), and hear the words of King David, who, much like us, had times of weariness and struggle.

The LORD is my shepherd; I shall not want.
He makes me lie down in green pastures.
He leads me beside still waters.
He restores my soul.
He leads me in paths of righteousness
    for his name's sake.
Even though I walk through the valley of the shadow of death,
    I will fear no evil,
    for you are with me;
    your rod and your staff,
    they comfort me.
You prepare a table before me
    in the presence of my enemies;
    you anoint my head with oil;
    my cup overflows.

Surely goodness and mercy shall follow me
all the days of my life,
and I shall dwell in the house of the LORD
forever.

So, friend, remind yourself you are secure in Christ. Continue to tell yourself these truths:

» God is faithful.
» God is with me.
» God redeems brokenness.
» God will work all things for my good.

There is a Japanese art of repairing broken pottery. The artists take and mend the broken pieces of pottery with lacquer mixed with powdered gold, silver, or platinum. They view the mended piece of pottery not as broken or worthless but actually as having more value than in its original state. The Japanese treat breakage and repair as part of the history of an object, giving it value and a story. Rather than viewing cracks as a disguise or an indication of a "less than" artifact, mending with gold adds value and character to the piece. Just as the pottery is mended with precious metal, this is a wonderful picture of the work God does in our lives.

See yourself as being mended with gold, fashioned to complete restoration. God can take the broken places of your life and, through His healing power, mend you with gold, truth, and love. He takes what we see as broken and builds us back into His original design for us. He doesn't see our cracks and pieces as worthless; He sees a vessel of honor, a woman made new, stronger, resilient, courageous, and rich in character and empathy. A gift to those around her.

The beauty in the breakage is that people can see Jesus. The broken places in our lives, when handed to God, can become a reflection of

His faithfulness and goodness. Our past experiences and pain can be transformed into a testimony to reflect our Creator and Healer. Our cracks and broken areas no longer limit us because through God's restoration, these areas confirm our call and mission to the world. This is the security we have in a good God. He can take the broken things and forge new and beautiful life.

Sometimes life can feel hard, whether it's a lost dream, a broken heart, or anything in-between; Jesus told His disciples in John 16:33 (NIV), "In this world, you will have trouble." I don't know about you, but I think, *Okay, that's not what I wanted to hear.* I'm being told I WILL have trouble. Honestly, I don't love that. I really don't. But that is the reality of the world that we live in. There is sin and evil in the world, and there is also free will; God doesn't control people. So, what do I do with that? The verse mentioned above does say that you will have trouble, but that statement is sandwiched between love. God has promised us peace in the middle of that trouble. John 16:33 (NIV) encourages us to take heart and realize that He has overcome the world:

"I have told you these things, so that in me you may have peace. In this world you will have trouble. But take heart! I have overcome the world."

You might be thinking, *That's great for eternity. I am so very, very thankful for that; I truly am, but I need help here. I need help now! I need something to help me live in this life that I must walk through here on earth now! I need Jesus now.*

The good news is that salvation is for eternity, but it's also for the here and now. God saved you so that someday you could live in heaven with Him forever, but that's not all He did. He also redeemed you. He gave you the righteousness of Jesus, and He put the Holy Spirit in you to act as a comforter, a guide, and a friend. The Holy Spirit . . . He is God in you. Jesus didn't leave you to navigate life alone; He gave you His Spirit. He is with you. He guides you, comforts you, and directs you. Yes . . . in your pain, trauma, and loss, God is with you. We were never promised a life without the trials and effects of evil in the world. But we were promised a God who would be with us through it.

So, even if it's broken, you can still be whole.

Even if they left, you are not alone.

Even if the job doesn't work out, God will lead you to where you need to be.

God is a God of redemption, the God of the turnaround, the comeback. Redemption wouldn't be possible if first there weren't pain, loss, or sin. This is what He means when He says He has overcome the world. Circumstances are facts of life. Facts are just that, details. And facts change. The Word of God never changes.

God's love and law supersede the facts and circumstances in the natural. God has OVERCOME the world. If we base our identity and value on God, our lives can look messy, and we can still have peace. Does that mean that I don't feel pain, loss, or grief? No, those trials and emotions still come, but I don't have to stay there. I can invite the Holy Spirit into those circumstances and allow Him to lead and guide me. God will work where I cannot and bring healing and truth to the broken places of my life.

Will He fix it all the way I want or expect? No, not usually. And it's hard to write that. I so badly wanted God to fix my life and put it back together like it was before it imploded. But for me, He didn't put it back to how it was. If He had done what I wanted, my life would have gone back to how it was before, and it would have led to the same downfall. Nothing would have changed, and I would have the same outcome.

God knew I needed change. I needed Him to work in me; I needed to be made new.

At first, this was disappointing. God not only didn't do what I wanted, He didn't even do (in my own misconception) what I thought a "good God" would do. Through trusting God (with some doubt) and walking forward, I saw that God did more than what I could have ever imagined. I wanted the facts of my life to change, but unfortunately, the past can't change. The facts didn't change, but my perception of them did. God's healing didn't undo what was done, but His healing changed the way I interpreted my life. That is the beauty of redemption; it supersedes the facts.

God redeemed me. He took me out of unhealthy patterns, belief systems, and relationships and set me on truth. He restored my heart. He healed my spirit, soul, and body. He gave me life, remade me, and set me free. I tell you all of this as a testimony of God's goodness—even in the trials of life. If He did it for me, He can do it for you. God's faithfulness is the safe haven in which we can live here and now. So, while John 16:33 might not be your favorite verse, you hold on to this promise and truth, and you will see the lining of hope that encapsulates the trials we face. The trials are preceded by peace and end with God overcoming the world, superseding circumstance.

We can't base our security, peace, joy, or contentment on positive circumstances. I don't know about you, but to me that feels like a tall order. When I've been operating a certain way my whole life, I am tempted to think that there really isn't another way. My process (good or bad) is to sit and struggle with it, to be mad at the situation, to be upset at sin in the world, and to tell God how I think it should be. I'm just being honest. After all, if we aren't honest with ourselves and God, we won't find true healing. After all of this, then I finally get to a place where I yield my opinion, feelings, and thoughts to the Almighty and say, *Okay . . . then show me Jesus. Show me how to live this life with security in You and not in my circumstances.*

God is faithful; when you open your heart and let Him in, He brings healing and truth. As I mentioned before, God works in many ways. Sometimes healing and perspective come through experiences that span a couple of weeks—but at one moment, they connect and make sense to me. Sometimes healing comes as a *knowing* deep in my heart. Other times, it's through a friend, a book, a blog, journaling, or thought.

Additionally, what I've learned is that understanding and healing often come after praise. After I get to a place in my heart where I feel like I'm at the end of me, and I can't figure this out, my heart cries, *I need You, Jesus,* and I find my heart in a posture of praise. This is a humble place, sometimes a frustrating place, but it's a place where I am yielded to God; I recognize my limited understanding and seek Him.

Let's be honest. We are all human; we will have feelings and reactions to the events of life, both positive and negative. But these events don't determine our contentment, joy, and peace. The idea is that my peace, joy, and contentment are outside of time, space, and circumstance. Contentment, joy, and peace are in a person, Jesus, and in a relationship with our heavenly Father. I am content because I know I am in Him. He is the One I run to in the high and low, and I know no matter what comes, I am safe if I am with Him. He is a place of peace . . . my safe haven. In the middle of trials and strife, in the middle of the victories and success, He is my safe place—I dwell in Jesus.

As Christians, we don't dwell in the world, in circumstances, trials, or even in our success. We dwell in the Almighty. The Bible says in Ephesians 2:6 that we are seated with Christ in heavenly places. We base our lives not on circumstances but on the unchanging love of God.

The redemption we have through Jesus, the forgiveness of our sins, and the power of the Holy Spirit living in us gives us security, peace, joy, and contentment.

Psalm 91 (ESV) says:

He who dwells in the shelter of the Most High
will abide in the shadow of the Almighty.
I will say to the LORD, "My refuge and my fortress,
my God, in whom I trust."
For he will deliver you from the snare of the fowler
and from the deadly pestilence.
He will cover you with his pinions,
and under his wings you will find refuge;
his faithfulness is a shield and buckler.
You will not fear the terror of the night,
nor the arrow that flies by day,
nor the pestilence that stalks in darkness,
nor the destruction that wastes at noonday.
A thousand may fall at your side,
ten thousand at your right hand,
but it will not come near you.
You will only look with your eyes
and see the recompense of the wicked.
Because you have made the LORD your dwelling place—
the Most High, who is my refuge—
no evil shall be allowed to befall you,
no plague come near your tent.
For he will command his angels concerning you
to guard you in all your ways.
On their hands they will bear you up,

lest you strike your foot against a stone.
You will tread on the lion and the adder;
     the young lion and the serpent you will trample underfoot.
"Because he holds fast to me in love, I will deliver him;
I will protect him, because he knows my name.
When he calls to me, I will answer him;
I will be with him in trouble;
I will rescue him and honor him.
With long life I will satisfy him
     and show him my salvation."

You might have just read that and felt a bit skeptical. That's okay. God will meet you where you are. I'm saying that from experience. God met me in my pain, sorrow, anger, and frustration. You might be thinking, *Well, that's nice and true for you, but God didn't protect me from rejection, pain, sorrow, grief, abuse, manipulation, etc.* I've been there too. I felt abandoned, rejected, and left exposed to evil and circumstance. I felt alone, isolated, and utterly unprotected by God. That was my view.

It was a hard space, and I want to acknowledge that I am truly sorry for the pain and loss you have experienced in your life. It was not fair. You did not deserve to be treated that way. It was harmful, and I see your pain. Our stories have different details, plots, characters, and endings, but my story, friend, is like yours. I wish we didn't experience the harsh effects of sin and our own or another's free will. This was something I had to come to terms with. We live in a fallen world; people, including you and me, have free will, and unfortunately, not everyone chooses kindness and love.

I cried out to God many nights. *Where are You? Help me . . . change this . . . change them.* And the beautiful yet frustrating thing God whispered was, *I'm here; I want to heal and change you.* God was with me through all the hurt and betrayal. I was always held, even when I didn't feel it, and God protected me in ways that I will never fully know. God showed me how He showed up through people He sent to me, ways in which He prepared me, and moments where He comforted me.

I didn't like the story I just lived. It was hard. It was painful, and in the same breath, I am SO thankful for what I've learned, how I've grown, and who I have become. God took my broken, shattered life and gave me a new foundation built on His love for me. He set me on solid truth, uprooted the lies, helped me learn and set boundaries, and made me new. He gave me His love, satisfied my soul, and brought me to His presence. He met me—rejected, wounded, hiding, and ashamed—and called me HIS. He saw me. And He sees you. He wants to rescue you from your pain, loss, and sorrow and heal your body, soul, and spirit. He wants to come close . . . to breathe the air you breathe and bring you into the light. He will do it. He is faithful.

So, when joy and good circumstances come, I dwell in and thank God for the blessings He brings. When bad news, hard trials, or negative circumstances come, I dwell in Him; I praise Him for who He is. Even though this event or circumstance isn't my preference, I know I am safe with God. I am safe under His wing. He is ultimately in control and will use this situation for my good and His purpose. He will protect, lead, and teach me in all things. He will heal me and set me on a solid foundation.

I am drawn back—continually— to Romans 8:28; it is so applicable and allows me to see I can trust God. No matter what comes my way, I can trust that God will take what the enemy meant for evil and turn it to good. Not all things are good. I acknowledge that and still don't like it . . . but I am a testament to the goodness and faithfulness of God. But I am a testament to the goodness and faithfulness of God. He took what happened in my life—what shattered me and was meant to destroy me—and used it to develop me, heal me, and set me on a mission to help others—to help you. While only you, my friend, know the depth and breadth of your pain, God is with you and loves you. If you let Him in, He can heal you beyond what you can imagine. He truly does bring beauty from ashes. Romans 8:28 (AMP) says so:

> *And we know [with great confidence] that God [who is deeply concerned about us] causes all things to work together [as a plan] for good for those who love God, to those who are called according to His plan and purpose.*

So, when I trust who is with me and in me, I don't fear circumstance. Yes—I'd prefer perfect positive situations. Who wouldn't? Truly, though, my relationship with God has grown the most in the valley. It was in that dark place that I learned to cling to my heavenly Father. I don't like pain, but what I've learned is that I am content even if it comes. I know God is faithful even in that hard place I might be walking through. What is happening isn't good, but I know deep in my soul that God will work it for my ultimate good. I will learn and grow and become stronger.

My spirit dwells with Him. My self-talk becomes, *I don't like this, God, but I trust You. I don't love this process, but I want what You want for me. This doesn't look good, Jesus, but Your Word says You will work all things for my good.* It is not denying reality and my feelings; it's acknowledging that this is happening. I recognize my feelings. I will address them to the One who can do something about them. *God, I'm taking them to You. You are God; I am not. You move, God. You lead me and heal me, Jesus. Show me the steps to take, and the rest I will leave to You.*

In this place, dwelling with the Lord, I find security, peace, joy, and contentment. He is the same yesterday, today, and forever. He is the Alpha and Omega, the beginning and the end. He is my comfort and rest. He is the peace in both the storms and calm of life. Peace, contentment, and joy are in a person. His name is Jesus. He is my safe haven here and now. Here are some verses that helped my heart settle on this truth:

And my God will meet all your needs according to the riches of his glory in Christ Jesus. —Philippians 4:19 (NIV)

And we know [with great confidence] that God [who is deeply concerned about us] causes all things to work together [as a plan] for good for those who love God, to those who are called according to His plan and purpose. —Romans 8:28 (AMP)

The Lord is my shepherd; I shall not want.

He makes me lie down in green pastures.

He leads me beside still waters.

He restores my soul.

He leads me in paths of righteousness
*   for his name's sake.*

Even though I walk through the valley of the shadow of death,
*   I will fear no evil,*
*   for you are with me;*
*   your rod and your staff,*
*   they comfort me.*

You prepare a table before me
*   in the presence of my enemies;*
*   you anoint my head with oil;*
*   my cup overflows.*

Surely goodness and mercy shall follow me
*   all the days of my life,*
*   and I shall dwell in the house of the Lord*
*   forever. —Psalm 23 (ESV)*

CHAPTER 10

Personal Healing— Personal God

I have found that God is personal; He is intimate. He created you, and He knows you. God speaks differently to each person. He knows your strengths and weaknesses and shows up specifically in ways that bring healing and wholeness to you and me. God made us, so He also knows what we need. When we pray, we often pray about what we want to happen or request our ideas of how God should move and work in our lives. Sometimes our requests are answered, and sometimes it appears as though they aren't.

Throughout my journey, God has answered many tangible prayers and shown Himself faithful. Yet He has also not answered some, or rather He has answered them in a way I wasn't expecting. In the middle of my journey, I was upset that God wasn't doing what I thought a "good God" should do. In hindsight, I'm glad that some of my prayers were "unanswered" (answered, yet not in the way I expected). And if you are honest with yourself, you can say the same. The relationship ended, but you realized it was for the better. You didn't get that job, but you kept your sanity. You get the picture.

The reality is that sometimes we don't get to see the miracle or answered prayer on this side of heaven. It's not that they were unanswered, but they were answered in a different way. This is hard to swallow. We often treat God as more of a genie than the unlimited, all-powerful God. We request and wish, hoping God does a miracle, and when He doesn't, we get upset. This is when we need to remember that we have a limited perspective, and God sees the end from the beginning. We need to remind ourselves that "God works all things for good for those who love Him and are called according to His purpose" (Romans 8:28, author paraphrase). Let me remind you again that not all things are good, and I see you. I've been there. I didn't think good could come out of my shattered situation and broken heart . . . but God.

||||||||||||||||||||||||||||||||||||||||||||||||||||||||||||||||||||||||||||||||||||||||||||

God is gracious in that He meets our needs and answers our prayers based on His view and plan; He knows what is good for us.

||||||||||||||||||||||||||||||||||||||||||||||||||||||||||||||||||||||||||||||||||||||||||||

God didn't answer some of my specific requests, but remember, God is God, and I am not. God sees and knows me better than I know myself; He also sees and knows others whom I am in a relationship with. Sometimes, God shows me His perspective. Other times, my "unanswered" prayers are God's way of protecting me. Often in a place of hurt and longing, we tend to want what is instant, or even the exact thing that was hurting us. God is gracious in that He meets our needs and answers our prayers based on His view and plan; He knows what is good for us. I have discovered that His will and protection over our lives are better than anything I can think or imagine (Ephesians 3:20).

I was in a season when I felt alone. I was walking a hard path after just having twins as the third and fourth kids in my family. I had just been told shattering news about my marriage, and I had a list of requests for God, regarding what I needed and what I thought He should do to fix the mess I was walking through. I remember crying in my bedroom night after night, asking God to show up, heal me, heal my husband, and bring us back together. I remember night after night God comforting me with His words and worship music, but I wanted action. I wanted tangible physical change in my life.

I'd like to say that happened, but it didn't. The nights continued, with fewer and fewer tears, more healing but still hurting. Still uncertain why things weren't changing, I wondered where God was in the mess I called my life. I was barely surviving, keeping my four little kids fed and clothed and feeding myself. God sent nanas, aunties, babysitters, and friends to support me over this time. He showed up in friendships, counselors, and spiritual mentors. I was absolutely surrounded by God's people, and I am so thankful for that. Yet, I was still so upset my prayers weren't being answered the way I'd hoped. God was answering me with what I needed—help from safe and loving people, healing to the core of my identity, love from the Creator of the world, and freedom to see the truth in a new light. I simply wanted a redeemed relationship, but God wanted to redeem me and my soul.

Fast-forward to today; life is different. It doesn't look at all like what I thought my life would or should look like. The structure from the outside still looks a little broken and tattered, but my life on the inside is flourishing and strong. The appearance of the trial is still present. A lot of what I had asked God for He didn't do, but some He did do. It is clear God is out to heal me but not in the way I thought. God is with me; I am learning and growing, constantly getting healthier as a person. After some clarity and more hurt in my marriage, I am now set on a new path. God has brought me to a new town, a new home, and a new direction in life.

I went to a worship night at my new church with a friend and was in a place of yielding and searching for God. And to say God brought healing is an understatement. He is so personal and amazing it's almost hard to fully explain in written words alone. I was praising and singing when God showed me a picture in my mind playing out like a movie. Jesus was running through my hallways with my kids, laughing; then suddenly, He was dancing with us in the living room, then eating dinner and talking with us, and finally sitting on my bed with my older boys and me as we read a story together. All these pictures in this movie or vision had happened over the past few weeks in my home. They were memories I had created with my children. Through that time, I had been asking God where He was . . . asking Him to show me where He was in these moments when I needed Him or thought I needed another adult in my home. He was faithful; He showed me.

Then an image flashed back to the memory I wrote about above. He showed me that room I had spent so many hours in crying and praying, and He showed me an image of Him there in the room with me the whole time. He was sitting by me, consoling me, as I poured out my tears and heart in writing, groaning, and prayers. Also, at the same time, He showed me He was outside the bedroom door, standing guard. Protecting me and keeping me safe. At that moment, what I thought came crashing down. I had been so upset over the past few years that God hadn't answered my prayers, but He had. He just answered them in a way I wasn't expecting.

Flashes of memory over these hard years started popping into my head. Each time I saw what "I had thought" was happening, and then Jesus showed me where He was and how He showed up. It was like the second cut of a movie where they add the computer-generated image over the scene that was just filmed. It was incredible. I saw Him holding my twin babies, playing and tickling their toes. I saw Jesus sitting with me on the couch . . . walking with me on the trail. I saw Him playing with my two older boys when I was unable to give them attention. He was with me in my car, during my counseling sessions, and with each step that I took forward. He answered my prayers, just not in the way I expected Him to, and I am so grateful.

We don't always see the answered prayer, and that can be challenging, but I truly hope that this example encourages you to know God is working on your behalf even when you don't see it, even when you don't feel it, and even when it doesn't match your preference. Our view as humans is so limited. We often want things that aren't the best for us. We can trust that if God isn't answering our prayers the way we want, He has something different and better for us. We need to trust that He is a good Father. He IS good. He is answering you and guiding you into His plan for you, according to Matthew 7:11 (AMP):

> *If you then, evil (sinful by nature) as you are, know how to give good and advantageous gifts to your children, how much more will your Father who is in heaven [perfect as He is] give what is good and advantageous to those who keep on asking Him.*

All my concerns and worries . . . He was already addressing them before I even spoke them aloud. He was helping me parent my kids, caring for my children, and sending physical help with dishes, clothes, cleaning, and feeding babies. God was with me in my tears, protecting me in times of deep pain and vulnerability. He was healing my identity and my heart. He was teaching me His ways of peace, joy, and rest. He wants to show you where He is in your life too. Ask Him. Ask Him to reveal Himself in a personal way to you. Friend, God is faithful. This is love like no other. Let Him in; let Him heal you.

To give you another example of how personal God is, let me tell you a story about Kelly. She and I were on a girls' trip to Florida with a few friends. Kelly had been dealing with a lot of anxiety and fear in her life. On the trip, she began to have panic attacks that she hadn't experienced in a few years. The first two days of our trip, Kelly was a little reserved and concerned, dealing with anxious thoughts about her health, her future, and her kids.

One day on the beach, I was very aware of Kelly's anxiety and rising fear. I decided to pray for her and walk in the water. This whole trip, I felt like God kept telling me, *I see you.* I didn't know exactly why He kept telling me that, but nonetheless, that was the impression I had. As I walked in the water, I started to view the ocean as God's love. We can't even fathom the vastness and depth of the ocean, and God's love is far greater than that. The waves continued to wash over my feet as I was walking along the shore, and it began to set in that God's grace and love are like the waves. They keep coming and crashing on the shoreline, covering me with water. It never stops; I have no control over it, and regardless of what I do, it keeps on coming.

After a few moments of praying, I felt the Holy Spirit give me an idea that could possibly help Kelly. The thought came to me: *Pick up a seashell for each and every thing that is causing fear or anxiety in your life. Be specific as you pick up each shell, and name the fear. Look at the ocean and view it as God's love. See the waves crashing on the shore as His grace and love washing over you. Then throw the fear or anxious thought into the ocean as an act of faith, releasing the fear, anxiety, and future* to God and His unlimited love. Once you throw it in, you will no longer be able to go in and find it or grab it; it's impossible with this amount of water, sand, and shells to still pick up the same one. Use this as a marked moment of trust . . . of submitting your fear and anxiety to God. He didn't design you to carry this weight. He wants you free. God is responsible; you are called to be obedient.

My next thought was, Will this really help? And honestly, maybe Kelly doesn't want any suggestions. But right after that thought came, so did Kelly; she came to stand next to me on the shoreline. I told Kelly what I had just heard in my spirit. She looked at me and said, "Okay, I'll do it." She walked up the beach on her own and had a marked moment with God. I decided to do the same thing and release the people and circumstances in my life to God as well. It was a marked moment, a holy presence, an act of faith. Kelly came back, I gave her a hug, and we carried on with our day at the beach. After that, nothing happened, and we went about our trip as normal; Kelly did seem a little "lighter" throughout the day.

Two days after we got home, Kelly called me to tell me that that moment on the beach shifted something inside of her. She felt different; she felt lighter. She hadn't realized how much she had let fear in and how much it was controlling her. That physical act of faith shifted the way she felt spiritually and even physically. She didn't have any more panic attacks, and she felt different. I had no idea a small thought God had given me on the beach would have such an impact on her. At that moment, it had seemed small and didn't feel spiritual.

She said that moments before I had talked to her on the shore that day, she had been crying out to God and asking if He even saw her. When she said that, I immediately started to cry. The whole trip, God had been telling me, I see you, I see you, I see you, over and over. I appreciated hearing that God saw me, but it wasn't until this moment (two days later) that I realized that those words were for Kelly. The exact thing she had been questioning, God had been speaking, and I had the opportunity to be the vessel He used to share His love.

God is so amazing; the English language doesn't have a word that does justice to explaining how cool God is. If you glean anything from this chapter, please hear this. God cares about you. God is a personal God, and He desires to speak to you, heal you, and be in a relationship with you. One of the names of God is *El Roi*, the God who sees me. God sees you, friend.

|||||||||||||||||||||||||||||||||||||||||||||||||||||||||||||||||||||||||||||||||||||||||||||||||||||||

God cares about you. God is a personal God, and He desires to speak to you, heal you, and be in a relationship with you.

|||||||||||||||||||||||||||||||||||||||||||||||||||||||||||||||||||||||||||||||||||||||||||||||||||||||

CHAPTER 11

A New MO

Submitting and yielding to God is hard. It goes against every grain in my human body which wants to control and know the future. Control is a four-letter word.

C-R-A-P (Control-Releases-Anxiety-and-Projection)

As I was considering what happens when we try to control our lives or circumstances in our lives, the word crap popped into my mind. It's not a word that is polite, and it doesn't even sound pleasant as you say it. Yet as I wrote it down, I saw the illustration and acronym God was showing me. When we try to control, we usually make a bigger "mess" of life by projecting and pushing personal agendas that leave us full of anxiety, fear, and in a loop of trying to get control.

Control is an illusion. It promises peace and serenity but is falsely rooted in idolatry and self-effort. The opposite of what Christ calls us to. Control takes God out of the picture and says, "I can do this, I know best, I know better than God." Control exhausts us because it is a never-ending cycle that can't be attained. If you have lived more than, say . . . five years, you know that you have very little control over anything in life.

When I get into cycles of control, it comes across as a safety mechanism. When I am afraid about the future or a certain situation, I fall into anxiety, projecting fear or false expectations of what I think should happen in my life. This leaves me turning, agonizing, and trying to push my own agenda, which can be motivated by fear, pain, or wrong motive.

Believe me when I say this. I lived a lot of my life trying to manage and control my emotions, others' emotions (impossible), my future, and even the circumstances around me. I thought I'd be swallowed whole by chaos and lack of peace if I lost control. But honestly, I was creating this lack of peace in my head and heart by all the panicked "role-play projections" and attempts to control the outcome of my life—all of which, let's be honest, never happened.

Have you been there? Maybe you know what I'm talking about, creating a fictitious conversation of what you would say, could say, or how something "should" play out in your life. Or maybe you do this in reverse; you ruminate over what happened and talk yourself through the options of what would have been better. You enter the "woulda-shoulda-coulda" mindset. I've done both, and neither is helpful. Life rarely goes how "I think" it should go. This should be a lesson to me right now to stop. To stop trying to figure it out. All this inner need for control is causing the stress and anxiety I fear. Honestly, this way of thinking is causing more anxiety in me than just walking out my life in a place of yielding and trusting in God.

It's been about four years, well thirty-four years, of God gently prompting me to rest, to yield to His plan, and to walk it out in the present. I can't tell you how many times people, friends, sermons, and even God has said to yield (or submit). To stop trying to figure it all out and trust Him. To trust God and His timing; Why is this so hard? Why do I have such resistance to this? Why don't I just listen and let go? I'm certainly not in control, nor can I be, except for myself.

I was walking on a trail one day near my house and struggling (venting) with God about all the trouble that was happening in my life. I was so frustrated and basically begging God to change my circumstance; it was clear, though, that God was out to change my heart.

I saw an uprooted tree along the trail. I felt like God said He was uprooting all the lies and false beliefs in my life. He was digging up the things that were keeping me from the truth, peace, and deep relationship with Him and others. It isn't a good feeling to be uprooted, pruned, and cut. It's hard and, honestly, it's a part I wish we could skip. And that was my honest thought; *I don't want to do that. That doesn't seem comfortable, ideal, or fun.* But God knows what I need more than I do. And He knew if He didn't uproot the lies I believed and the systems I participated in, I'd never be able to hold the truth.

I walked a little further and saw a red barn. There was a man outside applying new wood slats to the sides. You could see the fresh, natural brown wood between the red of the original barn walls. I felt as though it was a picture of God replacing and rebuilding me. This man reinforced the barn structure and made it new. Some parts He took down and replaced, and some He left. I had the impression of God saying, *I want to do this, I want to rebuild you, I want to give you a new life.*

As I walked forward, I was frustrated. You might think, *You are hearing from God, and He is promising you that He will rebuild you. Why are you so frustrated?* If you aren't thinking that, I am (as I write this four years later). I'm looking at myself and wondering, *Why didn't I get this deep-seated hope, joyfully let go, and trust God?* But I'm learning to look back at myself and have grace for the season I was in. I can't judge yesterday's choices with the wisdom I have today. I was not the same person, and you aren't either. Honestly, that Ashley just wanted her life fixed now; she wanted life to go back to how it was. At that moment, I was acting like I'd rather have a magic genie instead of a loving and personal God. You think I would have been blown away that God was showing me this promise of what He wanted to do for me, but I wasn't (cringe). I'm human here. Let's be real together. I didn't want to let go of what I wanted, what I thought my life should look like. My marriage and family were broken and shattered, and I wanted God to fix them how I envisioned.

|||||||||||||||||||||||||||||||||||||||||||||||||||||||||||||||||||||||||||||||||||||||||||||||||||||||

Submitting starts small and grows and builds until you find yourself in a place of yielding your whole heart to God.

|||||||||||||||||||||||||||||||||||||||||||||||||||||||||||||||||||||||||||||||||||||||||||||||||||||||

I kept hearing God say, *Let go. Let go.* I continued my walk, being honest with God, and as I walked over this small bridge, I saw the most beautiful, manicured lawn, at least three acres, all mowed and trimmed. It led up to a beautiful home you would imagine seeing in France. Beautiful patio, cute charm, and a feeling of comfort and peace. I thought, *I want this, God, not all of that You showed me back there.* I felt like God said, *You can have this, but you need to let go. This is the process.*

Okay. At this point, still reluctant and scared of letting go of my dreams and desires, I turned around and started heading back to my car. As I turned and walked back over the bridge—I kid you not—someone had written the words "let go" on the back of a trail sign. I just laughed and started to cry. *Okay, God, I'll let go.* And that small submitting (yielding) at that moment led to another, and another, and another of many moments like this. Submitting is a process of saying yes to God and laying down our own ways and effort. Submitting starts small and grows and builds until you find yourself in a place of yielding your whole heart to God. And friend, that is the most beautiful and peaceful place to live. It's a place of rest and trust.

Here I am, four years later, writing this story, and I am at another place in my journey that I want to control. Life is not what I thought it would be. Some things are better, and some areas still need work. I feel like I am in the stage of God replacing and restructuring me, like that old red barn the man was fixing. I went through the uprooting stage; I felt that, and I so badly want to get to the French country stage, yet I feel like God is showing me that we never fully arrive. There is always more with God—more to experience, more healing, more truth, more love. Life isn't about ending up at the beautiful French-styled home; it's about the journey with God that cycles through all the stages. We will have seasons of uprooting, rebuilding, and of manicured-lawn French country living. What I long for about the French country living stage is the serenity and peace about it. I feel that God is saying you can have that peace in all the stages because He is with you. In uprooting, you can have peace. In rebuilding, you can have peace.

So, when I get the feeling that this is taking too long, and I want to take matters into my own hands, I can release them and be at rest and peace, even in a season of uprooting because God is with me. I know He will rebuild me and bring me into the destiny He has for me. When anxiety and the need to control come, I also hear God gently (and consistently) prompting me to rest, submit, and yield to Him. It's a choice—a choice I make daily.

I hear Him saying, *You rest; I'll handle it.*

Jeremiah 29:11-13 (NIV) says God has plans for you and for me:

"For I know the plans I have for you," declares the LORD, "plans to prosper you and not to harm you, plans to give you hope and a future. Then you will call on me and come and pray to me, and I will listen to you. You will seek me and find me when you seek me with all your heart."

He is teaching me to trust and yield to Him. He is good, and He has good for me. What I see in the verses from Jeremiah is amazing. God is giving us a promise that His plans are good and will prosper us. Then He gives us direction: "Then you will call on me and come and pray to me, and I will listen to you. You will seek me and find me when you seek me with all your heart." I love that He knows us. I love that He gives us the promise before the directive. He knows we struggle. He knows we want to control and to know the future. He sees us and wants to show us a new way to live—the way of yielding to him.

In this place of yielding our lives and hearts to Him, we find rest, we find peace, and we find security. We find all the things we long for, all the things that control promises but can't give us. God wants us to live lives at rest. I love how the Amplified Bible states Matthew 11:29:

"Take My yoke upon you and learn from Me
[following Me as My disciple],
for I am gentle and humble in heart,
and YOU WILL FIND REST (renewal, blessed quiet)
FOR YOUR SOULS."

Isaiah 26:3 (AMP) is also a great promise for us:

*"You will keep in perfect and constant peace the one whose mind
is steadfast [that is, committed and focused on You—in both
inclination and character],*

Because he trusts and takes refuge in You
[with hope and confident expectation].

I believe that God wants to set you and me free from fear, anxiety, control, and unrest. You might be thinking, *Great. This is great. I want this, but how? You don't know what I'm feeling; you don't see my life. You don't know what I'm going through, and if I give up control, I'll be left a victim of my circumstances and stuck.* And if you're not as headstrong as I am, well then, I'll say it for you.

I did and often still struggle with this thought or emotion. My emotions and fear sometimes scream louder than I'd like, and my veins often course with anxiety. So, if I'm not controlling, anxious, and projecting scenarios, what do I do? What's my action? How do you yield and submit to God? Let me assure you that God will do it. He will lead you and guide you, just as Philippians 1:6 (ESV) says: "And I am sure of this, that he who began a good work in you will bring it to completion at the day of Jesus Christ."

However, here are some practical action steps you can take. This is not a formula; faith and relationships never are a formula. Yet I didn't want to leave you with these new ideas without some simple steps you can take to move forward.

Practical Step #1: Yield and Submit

Realize that God is in control, not you. It's His job to complete the work. God is responsible, and we are obedient. Renounce the lie that you must do it. The lie is: if I don't do x, y, and z, then nothing will happen. Tell yourself the truth like Philippians 1:6. Therefore, your first job is to yield and submit. Yield your self-effort. Self-effort can't earn you salvation, right standing, or even honor and favor. We fall short. We have a limited perspective. We are not God—and I am very thankful for that.

Yielding is saying: "This is hard; I don't like this, God, but Your will be done. This isn't what I thought, but You know the plans You have for me. I want what You have for me, Jesus. I submit my desires to You. Give me Your desires. Show me what to do." It's getting into a posture of humility and saying, "I've made a mess, God. I can't do this on my own. I need You." I'm stating this simply because it's simple. But it's not easy. It pulls at your humanness; it takes obedience and trust. It's a growing trust, and God builds it. Hear me: it has been a struggle but one that has proven to be filled with peace and joy.

Yielding and submitting doesn't mean you do nothing. Trust and faith still require you to move, live, and act. It's just that you are moving, living, and acting on the prompting of the Holy Spirit. You are living and moving in a posture of giving up what you want and will to God's will. The safest place to be is in the will of God. Yielding and submitting puts you there.

Yes, it still requires effort, but it's through God's strength that you move, not your own strength (which is limited). Yes, you still might have feelings and emotions that beg for control, but you have a choice in what wins out. Yielding and submitting still have action; faith is action-based. The difference is you are acting and moving in the grace and direction of God. He has the best plans for you, and you will find HIM—and His plan—when you seek Him with all your heart.

Practical Step #2: Connect

The second thing I've found that is important is connection. God desires to connect with you, to have a relationship with you. He delights in and wants to be in unity with you. Just like in chapter 8, God wants to have tea with you. Pour your heart out to Him, and let Him tell you what's on His heart. If you want to know God's will for you, dive into the Bible. Spend time reading, worshiping, listening, and journaling.

Just like any other relationship, trust is built over time, and part of submitting is trusting in whom you are following: His heart, His promises, and His timing. Trust is hard-won and developed over time. You might be thinking, *Oh, great, more time . . . more waiting,* but that's not necessarily true. God is beyond time. He can redeem you and your trust in Him in exponential ways as He expresses His love, heart, and plans for you. This time of connecting with God allows you to fix your focus on Him.

Matthew 6:33 (BSB) states, "But seek first the kingdom of God and His righteousness, and all these things will be added to you." If you connect with and focus on God, He will take care of the rest. Yes, you are still called to walk forward in life, but with your eyes focused on Jesus, you can be sure He will lead you where you need to go.

Though I struggled on my journey, submitting to God has redeemed my trust, my view, and my perspective of Him over twenty years in an instant. Let me explain. This comes from the story of the worship night at my church. Not only did God show me how He answered my prayer, He used this experience to reestablish my trust in Him.

As mentioned previously, after awakening me to His presence in my daily life, God showed me a picture, continuing like an old movie, of myself in high school. I saw Jesus was with me, but He was walking three steps behind me. It was like He was patiently following me. I had ideas, dreams, and plans that I could achieve through self-effort. This was not a scolding that I felt. He was showing me He was there, but I was trying to control my life and choices. I wasn't yielded to Him.

He was with me, I saw His protection and guidance, but I was head-strong. "I" had the plan and executed it without concerning Him. He showed me where He guided, prompted, and protected me, but also how He didn't force me to yield. He doesn't make us submit. Was He with me? Absolutely. Was He sovereign? Yes. While He allowed me to carry on this way, He was always protecting and present.

I stopped at that moment, after seeing this movie in my mind, in awe of God. My perspective up until that point was of confusion, frustration, and loss. I felt like I couldn't see God and was questioning if I could truly trust Him—with all of me. But at that moment, it all shifted. It was as though He took my perspective of the previous twenty years and showed me His. All my ups and downs, losses and victories were overlayed with His presence and truth. He healed my heart from lies I had believed based on my experiences and truly reestablished twenty years of trust in that one night. God is so good. And so faithful. I'm literally in awe of His love for me.

God desires to heal you, connect with you, and build trust in you. I see the respect God gives us as His children; He doesn't demand or push His way in. He prompts, guides, leads, and waits for us to choose to yield to Him and to be open to His way of life. God desires good for us. He has good plans. And those good plans start with connection and relationship with Him.

Practical Step #3: Rest

Rest is something that I am constantly waiting for, hoping for, pushing through until . . . but it's short-lived and never fully satisfying. Like a 24-hour break, it's a short vacation until life starts again. This type of rest does nothing but help us escape. I think that God wants us to see rest differently, to see rest as a state of being, not a break from life. He wants rest to be our MO, a way of life: body, soul, and spirit at peace and rest.

Rest isn't necessarily what you think; it takes work. I've learned that rest is actually active. It's an active awareness of where your body, soul (mind, will, and emotions), and spirit are. Rest is a constant entering into—a way of being rooted in the present moment. Unhooking from the past, all the triggers and memories, and unhooking from the future, anxiety, and projection. It is submitting and moving from a state of doing to a state of being. Rest is the gift that God wants to give us.

Resting in Christ requires yielding/submitting and trust. Rest is continuing to be in a humble mindset. I am not God, and I release the outcome of my life to Jesus. I yield and submit; Jesus is responsible, and I am obedient. My hands are open with my heart in a posture of aligning to God. Rest is trusting that God has got it. That He is in control, and I am not. It releases me of the inner drive to fix and work things out; it leaves me in a beautiful state of presence and trust.

As I am learning what rest is and is not, I find that it's sometimes hard to explain. It's not what the world or our natural minds think of it. It is a state of being. Below is a section of my journal. As I wrote, I felt God speaking these words to me about rest. Be enveloped in His love, in His presence, and under the shadow of His wing.

Picture God telling you this:

I want you to rest.

Rest in knowing I have plans for you for good. (Jeremiah 29:11)

Rest in knowing you can trust Me. (Proverbs 3:5-6)

Rest in knowing I am taking care of it. (Romans 8:28)

Rest in knowing it's coming.

Rest and be in this present moment. (Psalm 16:11)

Rest in knowing I'll give you the next step. (Psalm 119:105)

Knowing it's handled.

Knowing My love.

Knowing you hear Me. (John 10:27-28)

Knowing you take the next step.

Rest.

I have begun a good work in you, and I will bring it to completion. (Romans 8:28)

Rest.

Stop striving.

Start living out of My rest. Move and breathe.

Just be.

Rest is worship.

Rest is trust.

In My rest (presence), you will find My fullness of joy. (Psalm 16:11)

Rest is not inactive.

It's moving, living, and loving from a place of trust, worship, yielding, grace, self-acceptance, and peace.

Rest My child—"For I know the plans I have for you," declares the Lord. "Plans to prosper you, and not to harm you, plans for hope and a future." (Jeremiah 29:11, author paraphrase)

Rest is your word.

It's not the absence of doing.

It's the absence of anxiety, fear, and rumination.

Rest is living in the present, forgiving, grieving, and letting go of the past.

Dreaming for the future—but trusting (not projecting) that you are on the right path.

Rest is active.

You need to enter it. (Hebrews 4:10)

Rest requires you to seek peace. (Psalm 34:14)

To seek Me. (Jeremiah 29:13)

Rest requires presence and awareness.

In HIS presence is the fullness of joy.

Come to the well and rest.

Rest is holy ground—communion with Holy Spirit.

Rest is a relationship.

Rest is talking to Jesus.

Sitting with Jesus.

Listening to Jesus.

Rest says, "I can't do this on my own. . . . I invite you, Holy Spirit, in."

Rest yields.

Rest co-labors with God. (1 Corinthians 3:9)

Rest puts the responsibility on God and leaves us to hear and obey.

Rest is a dance. . . .

Sometimes we step off beat, but God calls us back into rhythm with Him.

Rest is a flow.

Rest brings grounding, comfort, and peace—like a weighted blanket
that wraps you in security, warmth, trust . . . a knowing.

Rest is where you are meant to live.

Rest is where I want you to stay.

When you find yourself spiraling, enter back into My rest.

Rest is intimacy, trust, and comfort with Jesus.

Rest is a choice; it's a practice.

Be present. Let go of the past, and stop grasping for the future.

Just be.

Rest is freedom. (2 Corinthians 3:17)

It's a practice, entering into rest. It takes time and repetition to create
a "new normal." Breathing or riding a bike becomes an involuntary

action led by muscle memory; the goal is to make presence, resting, and yielding to God, an involuntary action, a way of being. It takes repetition to become automated. Remember, God will lead us; He will do it. We just get to listen and obey.

Practical Step #4: Praise

Another key step in submitting and yielding to God is praise. When life is going well and it's my idea of good, I'm all for praise and thankfulness. It's when life is hard and challenges arise that I struggle to praise. My natural tendency is to worry or complain. Over and over in the Bible, it says to come to God with your cares and worries; He wants to hear them. He wants to help. However, the thing I'm noticing—and it's emphasized below—is that it says to come to God with thanksgiving:

> *Enter his gates with thanksgiving and his courts with praise; give thanks to him and praise his name. For the* LORD *is good and his love endures forever; his faithfulness continues through all generations. —Psalm 100:4-5 (NIV)*
>
> *Do not be anxious about anything but in every situation, by prayer and petition, with thanksgiving, present your requests to God. —Philippians 4:6 (NIV)*
>
> *Devote yourselves to prayer, being watchful and thankful. —Colossians 4:2 (NIV)*
>
> *Rejoice always, pray continually, and give thanks in all circumstances; for this is God's will for you in Christ Jesus. —1 Thessalonians 5:16-18 (NIV)*
>
> *The* LORD *is my strength and my shield; in him my heart trusts, and I am helped; my heart exults, and with my song I give thanks to him. —Psalm 28:7 (ESV)*

Praise changes my heart and perspective from frustration to gratitude. Praise lifts the name of Jesus. It positions me in a place of humility and thankfulness and reminds me of who God is and what He has already done. When I'm tired, frustrated, broken, and in the pit, praising and thanking Jesus is the last thing I feel like I want to do, but it's exactly what I need. It changes the atmosphere, and it changes my heart. Praise is also an act of obedience—submitting and yielding. It's often expressed as a posture of our hearts, minds, and bodies. My position of humility realigns me to God, His will, and His purpose.

Praise is strength: "Through the praise of children and infants, you have established a stronghold against your enemies to silence the foe and the avenger" (Psalm 8:2, NIV). It is often associated with worship songs. These songs often are straight out of Scripture which is a weapon we wield in the spiritual battle of life. Hebrews 4:12 (ESV) :

For the word of God is living and active, sharper than any two-edged sword, piercing to the division of soul and of spirit, of joints and of marrow, and discerning the thoughts and intentions of the heart.

God also says, "So shall my word be that goes out from my mouth; it shall not return to me empty, but it shall accomplish that which I purpose, and shall succeed in the thing for which I sent it" (Isaiah 55:11, ESV). That is what we do when we praise. We lift the name of Jesus, declare His words and promises over our lives and ourselves, and send His word into the world to do His will. We position our hearts in humility and thankfulness, and through all this, God changes our perspective. He resets our hearts to His. There is power in praise.

So, if you are in the process of learning to submit and don't know how or what's next if you want to enter rest . . . you praise. Instead of worrying, praise. Instead of ruminating on the past, praise God for what He has done and what He has brought you through. Remind your soul of how God saved you, redeemed you, remade you, loved you, and comforted you. Praise God for His promises, declare truth over your life and future, and "call those things that are not as though they were" (Romans 4:17, ASV). We praise; God moves and works in our lives: "And I am sure of this, that he who began a good work in you will bring it to completion at the day of Jesus Christ" (Philippians 1:6, ESV).

Practical Step #5: Listen and Obey

In a place of submission to God and His plan, you are no longer in control. This is great. You can rest and live life in the trust of Jesus. Remember, God is responsible; you are called to be obedient. What does this mean essentially? It means that you can trust that God is with you, that He has good plans for you, and that the Holy Spirit will guide you. This allows you to rest, knowing that God will take care of the future, and you can fully live in the present. After all, you can't live in the future—or the past for that matter. The present moment is the only reality there is. When you stop projecting, stop fearing the future, and stop trying to control outcomes (that you can't control anyway), your new mode of operating becomes listening to the prompts of God and obeying where He leads you.

Listening and obeying can begin practically. There are many guides and boundaries God gives us in the Bible. The Bible is a guide to life, not a list of rules, but a list of boundaries that allow us as God's children to live in freedom. You can also begin to listen to the Holy Spirit. If you have accepted Jesus as your Savior to forgive your sins, cleanse you, and be the Lord of your life, you have the Holy Spirit living in you. He is your advocate, a counselor. John 14:26 (ESV) says, "He [the Holy Spirit] will teach you all things." Have you ever been in a sticky situation, and you have that gut feeling? That's the Holy Spirit. Have you ever had an intuition about your job, circumstance, or friend? That is the Holy Spirit. We like to name the Holy Spirit fate, chance, luck, intuition, or a gut feeling, but the reality is most of that is God.

|||||||||||||||||||||||||||||||||||||||||||||||||||||||||||||||||||||||||||||||||||||||||||||||||||||||||

The Bible is a guide to life, not a list of rules, but a list of boundaries that allow us as God's children to live in freedom.

|||||||||||||||||||||||||||||||||||||||||||||||||||||||||||||||||||||||||||||||||||||||||||||||||||||||||

Have you ever been in the middle of a problem, and a solution just "popped" into your mind? That's God. He is consistent with His character, so if you have the idea to steal, lie, cheat, or betray—it's not God, not the Holy Spirit. You get the idea; God is speaking to His people all the time. Sometimes, we give Him credit, and sometimes we take the credit. Listening is beginning to notice the prompts of the Holy Spirit in your life and responding in obedience. It's living in God's knowledge and will instead of trying to do it on our own.

I don't know about you, but Proverbs 3:5-6 (ESV), "Trust in the LORD with all your heart, and do not lean on your own understanding. In all your ways acknowledge him and he will make straight your paths," takes the pressure off. This allows me to let go . . . truly be at rest . . . and live free in the freedom God intended. I am not responsible for the outcome; God is. This doesn't give me license to sin or be irresponsible. I am still responsible for myself and my choices, but I am now in a position of yielding to God's prompting. God calls us to co-labor with Him:

> For we are God's fellow workers [His servants working together]; you are God's cultivated field [His garden, His vineyard], God's building. —1 Corinthians 3:9 (AMP)

God leads; we follow. God speaks; we move. My job is now to listen, then follow through. God is responsible for the future. I am called to be obedient to His ways, His call on my life, and His prompts. Galatians 2:20 (AMP) tells me why and how:

> I have been crucified with Christ [that is, in Him I have shared His crucifixion]; it is no longer I who live, but Christ lives in me. The life I now live in the body I live by faith [by adhering to, relying on, and completely trusting] in the Son of God, who loved me and gave Himself up for me.

When we submit ourselves to God, He then lives and shows His love through us. He is Lord over our hearts, minds, bodies, and spirits. When we listen and obey God's prompts, we are the hands and feet of Jesus. When you help your family, it's Jesus moving your hands—Jesus washing dishes, packing lunches, and cleaning your house. It's Jesus's love when you help a friend in need, call to give support, or show up with a meal. Jesus in you. God's job is the leading and prompting. Our job is the yielding, listening, and obeying. Again, it's a dance. It's a picture of flowing with the Holy Spirit in you. God is always here, always working, and always available. It's our job to be aware of His presence, to hear Him, and act on His leading. We listen and obey; it's simple but not always easy.

CHAPTER 12

Contentment

C ontentment has been an area of growth for me for many years. After walking through the hardest season of my life, I just wanted perfect peace and circumstances. I wanted God to show up and right all the wrongs—hey, even go back and change the past if He could and would. I didn't like the brokenness I was living and carrying. Life didn't seem fair. God was asking too much of me, and the world was taking too much from me. Can't life just be easy, can't we just have peace, and can't people just be kind? Can't You just fix these circumstances, God? I've had many conversations with God, asking Him to switch circumstances, fix hearts, and erase the facts of life. Well . . . He didn't. And honestly, now I'm glad He didn't. If He had, I'd still be floundering in anxiety. I'd be discontent, owned by the ups and downs of life.

Have you been there: desperate for reprieve and change, and you don't get it . . . wondering how you can be content with this season, this trial, this job, this situation? Let's all be honest; sometimes, we'd like a month-long vacation to the Cayman Islands or Hawaii. But even a place as peaceful and beautiful as the ocean cannot bring true contentment to your soul. Have you ever heard anyone say, "You can't run away from your trouble because anywhere you go, it's there with you"?

I'm taking a long journey with contentment. I'm learning in bits and pieces . . . my heart still desiring positive circumstances . . . my spirit continuing to remind me of truth. My contentment cannot be based on circumstances because if it is, I will lose my peace and stability. It's shifting sand. It's just like the Bible song: "A foolish man built his house upon the sand. The winds and rain came down, and the floods came up, and the house went splat." Sand is not a firm foundation. The song also says, "A wise man built his house upon the rock (Jesus), the winds and rain came down, and the floods came up, and the house on the rock stood firm." In both situations, the winds blew, the rain fell, and the floods rose, but one house fell and the other stood strong. This is a picture of contentment, stability, and a firm foundation.

My contentment is based on Jesus.

It's based on knowing I am loved fully by my Father (God).

I'm forgiven completely.

God is within me (Holy Spirit). I am never alone.

So, if I'm in deep water, He is with me.

If the winds blow, He is with me.

If I'm on the mountain top, He is with me.

My contentment is in Him. It doesn't ignore the realities of life; it supersedes them. I do not ignore trials and emotions, but I also don't let them control me. I address emotion; I address trials and issues. I work through my pain and tell myself the truth about who I am. God is with me in the pit and in the victory. He helps me process both.

By no means am I saying that you should stay in and be content in all situations. In some situations, God calls us to stay—to stand and set boundaries. Abuse—physical, emotional, or spiritual—is never okay. I want you to hear that. I am not saying to hunker down and bear it. I do not stand for abuse, and neither should you. Boundaries are very important in life, and again, we do not ignore the issues in our lives and relationships. We face them, change, grow, and heal toward health. And God is with you in that fiery journey. You can have contentment and peace walking through it, and I am a testament to that.

It takes courage to say no, set a boundary, and take care of yourself. You should do these things to protect your body, soul, and spirit. If you are finding yourself in a situation where you are tolerating or trapped in abuse, ask for help. Call a pastor, mentor, or counselor who can help you take steps to protect yourself and heal. God is with you. He wants you safe. He will give you peace as you seek Him and His steps toward healing.

Contentment is not tolerating abuse or toxic patterns and relationships. Contentment is knowing whose and who you are in Christ and taking steps to be healthy and strong. It doesn't need a perfect circumstance but a perfect Savior. Therefore, the contentment and satisfaction of the soul can be present in the highs and lows of life. It's actually not based on a physical position or circumstance but the position of a person's heart and focus on God.

||||||||||||||||||||||||||||||||||||||||||||||||||||||||||||||||||||||||||||||||||||||||||||||||||

Contentment is not tolerating abuse or toxic patterns and relationships. Contentment is knowing whose and who you are in Christ and taking steps to be healthy and strong.

||||||||||||||||||||||||||||||||||||||||||||||||||||||||||||||||||||||||||||||||||||||||||||||||||

So, let's take a look at what Paul said to help us process this. What did Paul know? What was the key to his contentment? We can take some hints from his letter to the early church:

Rejoice in the Lord always. I will say it again: Rejoice! Let your gentleness be evident to all. The Lord is near. Do not be anxious about anything, but in every situation, by prayer and petition, with thanksgiving, present your requests to God. And the peace of God, which transcends all understanding, will guard your hearts and your minds in Christ Jesus.

Finally, brothers and sisters, whatever is true, whatever is noble, whatever is right, whatever is pure, whatever is lovely, whatever is admirable—if anything is excellent or praiseworthy—think about such things. Whatever you have learned or received or heard from me, or seen in me—put it into practice. And the God of peace will be with you. . . .

I am not saying this because I am in need, for I have learned to be content whatever the circumstances. I know what it is to be in need, and I know what it is to have plenty. I have learned the secret of being content in any and every situation, whether well fed or hungry, whether living in plenty or in want. I can do all this through him who gives me strength. —Philippians 4:4-9 and 11-13 (NIV)

Paul encouraged the Philippians to rejoice because God is near; He is close. They were not alone. The God of the universe was with them. This, in itself, should bring us to a posture of rejoicing. Like the Philippians, we have help and comfort. We have the Great Physician. And we have the Holy Spirit in us.

Paul then went on to tell them not to be anxious but to pray, and God's peace would guard their hearts and minds. I don't know about you, but I'll take the peace of God over my anxiety. I'll take the peace of God over perfect circumstances. I've had many times in my life where things have seemed almost perfect, and I've been anxious. I've had terrible moments of brokenness and pain, and God brought me peace that truly transcended life's circumstances.

The key here is to pray and present to God your requests with thanksgiving. We are not begging, complaining, or giving God our list of preferences or suggestions. We are coming with reverence and thankfulness for who He is. We know we are positioned in His love and favor, and we are asking God to move and do HIS will in our lives. We place our cares and worries at the feet of Jesus. We submit (again) our will and our plans to Him. We know we cannot do this on our own. And in exchange, He grants us His peace. It's as if we are hiding under the shadow of his wing. We have taken refuge in Him.

Paul then called the Philippians—and he calls us—to fix our thoughts and eyes on truth. My thoughts and mind can be in a thousand different places a day. Some thoughts I resonate with, and some come at me from my blind spot, and I think, *What was that?* I learned much over the past four years:

1) Not all my thoughts are true.

2) Not all my thoughts are helpful.

3) My thoughts are not me.

4) I get to choose what stays and what goes.

Let's fix our thoughts, eyes, and minds on what is pure, lovely, holy, and true. What do you do when thoughts arise that give you anxiety? Renounce them. Give them to God. Pray and ask Him what the truth is about that thought or situation. Find scripture, and pray it over yourself. Sometimes we need to remind our souls of the truth and let the Holy

Spirit lead. Your brain and its past memories and thoughts don't get to control you.

Then Paul closed by reminding the Philippians that God would meet their needs. Paul knew; he knew God was with him, wouldn't leave him, and would guide and provide for him. He was convinced of this. So, if he was in a rough situation, he praised. If he was on a mountaintop of victory, he praised. He knew no matter what, God would provide what he needed when he needed it. This is trust; this is contentment.

Let's recap Philippians 4:

1) Rejoice.

2) Be aware that God is with you.

3) Don't be anxious; instead, pray WITH THANKSGIVING!

4) Trust God—Worship and praise.

5) REST.

6) GOD will guard your heart and mind.

7) God will provide ALL your needs according to the riches of HIS glory.

Fifteen years ago, I traveled to Guatemala for a semester in college. It was an amazing experience, and even now, all these years later, God is reminding me of some of the lessons and pictures He gave me way back then. I'm reminded of the small village of Magdalena in the mountains where I was able to live and serve at a nearby school. The houses were made of cinder blocks; the floors were made of dirt. Most homes had one or maybe two rooms, and rarely did they have plumbing. Here we were, twenty-year-old students from the United States coming to serve this community, and I believe they impacted and taught me more than I served them. The people of Magdalena showed me a picture of contentment.

I've never seen such joy and contentment amidst such poverty. I've also never witnessed such generosity and love without much means. The people graciously helped us learn Spanish and gave up one of their rooms (with five members of their own family) to let us live with them. They fed us, taught us, and went to church with us. They welcomed us into their families and hearts. They lived in very hard situations but had the most joy I have ever seen. They were content and settled. They knew Jesus; they were at rest. It showed me that contentment has little to nothing to do with circumstance. It has everything to do with Jesus and a heart of gratitude. It was a humbling experience to see peace and rest rooted in truth.

CHAPTER 13

Joy

I have been told that joy and contentment go hand in hand, and now I believe it. Both joy and contentment are found outside of circumstance and in a person, Jesus. If you don't see the trend, well, you'll eventually get it; it's JESUS. Since beginning this journey, I have discovered that joy does not come and go with the highs and lows of life.It is not something you can buy or create because it is a gift deep-seated in your soul. Joy is often equated with happiness or a happy feeling, but happiness is dependent on circumstances. Joy is not. Joy can often be partnered with happiness, but it's not always accompanied by a positive feeling. Sometimes joy is reflected as hope and truth. It can sit alongside sadness or grief and still hold you in peace, hope, and faith. Joy is a state of being that is centered on who Jesus is and the high truth of His complete love for us.I can have joy even while walking through challenging trials.

Joy is a lens through which we look: the lens of the Father's eyes, what and whom He sees. Joy is seeing through a lens of love; it's seeing Jesus. This is why joy can sit right next to fear or sorrow and stand firm—it doesn't ignore the realities of life; it encompasses and supersedes them.

Joy is basking in the Father's love for us, allowing His love to fill us and be our source. Joy is the knowledge that though it may sit next to happiness, sorrow, strength, anger, or fear (at different parts of life), God is faithful, God is for me, and God loves me. And He promised to work all things for the good of those who love Him and are called according to His purpose (Romans 8:28). Not all things in life that happen are good, but He promises that He will work all things for good. We will grow, learn, mature, and deepen our faith, and He will awaken our hearts to His truths. Joy is a lens of seeing life through Jesus. James 1:2-4 (NIV) makes this clear:

> *Consider it pure joy, my brothers and sisters, whenever you face trials of many kinds, because you know that the testing of your faith produces perseverance. Let perseverance finish its work so that you may be mature and complete, not lacking anything.*

> Joy is basking in the Father's love for us, allowing His love to fill us and be our source. Joy is the knowledge that though it may sit next to happiness, sorrow, strength, anger, or fear God is faithful, God is for me, and God loves me.

The Bible also says that "the joy of the Lord is [my] strength" (Nehemiah 8:10, NKJV), and "in [HIS] presence there is fullness of joy" (Psalm 16:11, ESV, emphasis added). What I hear from these verses is that there is joy in God's presence, and there is strength in joy. Therefore, I am made strong in the presence of God. Logically, we can then say that joy and contentment are not in life's circumstances but in a relationship with and the presence of God. Now, we are temples of the Holy Spirit. After Jesus died and was raised to life and ascended into heaven, He sent us the Holy Spirit to dwell in us. So, the presence of the living God is in us! Joy and strength are in us. God is with us; He will never leave us. His presence is here now! The question is, *Am I in the present with God? Am I aware of Him, listening and watching for what He is doing in me and my life?*

Sometimes the noise and fast pace of life set me on course to either be planning four weeks ahead, ruminating about what happened yesterday, or scrolling to see what the rest of the world is up to. Presence takes time and space and requires me to slow down. In our day and in this culture, we have FOMO—Fear of missing out. It's a real thing. We are concerned if we turn off social media, silence our phones, or take time to rest, we will miss out and somehow be left behind. These emotions are real, but the reality is that they're keeping us from the truth and from time spent with God.

Sometimes, silence is deafening; it's hard, and it can feel painful. I just walked through a season where I was stuck home for weeks: kids sick, plans canceled, life halted. Then I felt Holy Spirit tell me to stop scrolling on social media. I was utterly alone (except for my four little kids), myself, and the Holy Spirit. The silence made me want to crawl out of my skin; I wanted to escape. I felt panicked and left alone to face my fear of aloneness and loneliness.

With the noise off, comparison shut down, and no outside influ-ence, I had a lot of time—to think, to listen, to process, and to wait on God. And waiting is HARD. In the waiting, I saw my lack of joy and contentment. I wanted to grasp the next thing, move forward, and keep pushing on. But that is not the gift God wanted to bring to me. He wanted to bring joy, contentment, and rest.

In His presence is truly the fullness of joy; that is what I experienced as I walked thirty-one days of focus, thirty-one days of silencing the world, and thirty-one days of house arrest due to illness. Joy didn't come right away. Not going to lie; I was mad and upset; cue toddler tantrum in my head. It came with reluctance, frustration, and finally submitting. However, God was speaking, even when I was frustrated. I heard His voice and was led to books, sermons, and words He was speaking to me.

When I hit the place of submitting and rest, I felt a flow of words straight to my soul. His presence felt tangible, and yes, the joy started to flow. Before that, His presence was there; I'm sure of it. I was just unaware or resistant to it. This was when I began having tea with Jesus each night, practicing, listening, and asking Jesus questions. As I spent that time each night, I truly saw the joy in Jesus. His lightheartedness, love for me, care about my life, and His truth. I began to hear Him speaking not just at our "Teatime" but in the car, at the grocery store, and when I was playing with my kids. I was starting to recognize the voice of God and His promptings throughout my day. It brought peace and joy to my heart; I truly felt seen and known. I felt His presence. To know something on a mental level is one thing, but to experience it is to put that knowledge in our hearts.

Enter His rest, His presence, and His joy. His is the love that you have longed for. It's the real thing.

CHAPTER 14

Come to the Well

*I*t's possible that you are still here, nearing the end of the book and wondering, *Is this for me?* You might think you don't know me, what I've done, or what's been done to me. If so, I want to introduce you to a character in the Bible. She doesn't have a name which I think is purposeful. She is called the Samaritan woman or the woman at the well.

Let's start with some backstory. I encourage you to read about her. Open the Bible or search the internet for John 4:1-42, and read the story of the Samaritan woman. I think we can resonate with her story and life. You read it, and then, let's unpack it together.

When Jesus met the woman at the well, she was set up for failure. She was a Samaritan, not a Jew. This already denotes that she was an outsider. She didn't belong. Not only that, verses 19 and 20 say she wanted to worship God, but the Jews said the only place to worship God was in the temple in Jerusalem. So first, she is an outsider and second, she is restricted by culture. Jews didn't associate with Samaritans, and especially men didn't associate with Samaritan women. She was skeptical, and sometimes we are as well.

Not only was this woman culturally and religiously "not right," but she was also socially struggling. It says in the Bible that Jesus sat down at noon at the well. Most women at this time would have come to the well in groups in the cool of the night or in the early morning. This woman came alone, in the middle of the day, in isolation. Maybe she felt shame. Maybe she felt unworthy and unwanted. Have you been there? I have. She chose isolation, and if I'm being honest, when I feel shame, I choose isolation as well. Instead of facing my circumstances, self, or judgment from others, I hide. I pull back. Mostly it's out of self-protection, but it's not actually protecting me; it is hurting me. Isolation breeds depression, numbness, and more isolation. Sometimes the things we do to protect ourselves end up locking our pain away instead of healing it.

In the passage, Jesus asked the woman for a drink from the well; she was more than likely annoyed or resentful due to religious, cultural, and social disqualification and told Jesus why she was disqualified to do so. Again, I can see myself here, telling God, others, or myself why I'm not enough. This is why I love that Jesus went through Samaria. I love that He met this woman here at the well. I love that He came just for her. I love that through this story, Jesus broke molds and boxes we put ourselves and each other in. I love that Jesus showed God's love outside of cultural norms, religious rules, and self-effort. Then Jesus told her she should ask HIM for water in John 4:13-14 (MSG):

> *"Everyone who drinks this water will get thirsty again and again. Anyone who drinks the water I give will never thirst—not ever. The water I give will be an artesian spring within, gushing fountains of endless life."*

To be skeptical is an understatement; to not understand is natural. What, after all, was He saying? What inside of us thirsts for a solution that never runs dry? He was speaking to that space inside of all of us that is a God-sized hole that only He can fill. It houses a longing to be seen, known, and loved. Jesus saw the woman questioning and began to talk about her life. I love that Jesus, without condemnation, called her out for the life that she had led. Who knows the reason she had been married five times or why the man she was living with wasn't her husband? I am neither in a place to judge nor would I want anyone to judge me for my circumstances. Maybe she was left, betrayed, or abandoned. Maybe she made mistakes. It doesn't tell us, and that's not important.

The point is that Jesus included her:

"But the hour is coming, and is now here, when the true wor-shipers will worship the Father in spirit and truth, for the Father is seeking such people to worship him. God is spirit, and those who worship him must worship in spirit and truth."

The woman said to him, "I know that Messiah is coming (he who is called Christ). When he comes, he will tell us all things."

Jesus said to her, "I who speak to you am he." —John 4:23-26 (ESV)

Despite her race, culture, and religious restrictions and despite her past and present circumstances, Jesus chose her. He showed her there was new life and water that never ran dry. She had a physical need, and He met it on a practical and spiritual level. He said she was in. She belonged, and I believe God is saying that to you. You, friend, are in. God wants you. He sees you broken and damaged, scarred and dis-carded by people and the world, and He still calls you chosen, loved, and enough. He wants you.

⸻

Come to the source of all healing,
love, forgiveness, and power.
Come to Him and find your rest.

⸻

God is crossing borders and cultural norms to get to you. It doesn't matter what you've done or what was done to you. It doesn't matter your race, gender, economic status, or culture. It doesn't matter your past or your present. He loves you. He is asking you to come to the well. Come to the source of all healing, love, forgiveness, and power. Come to Him and find your rest. If you are waiting for a sign, here it is. He is calling you. Yes, you.

CHAPTER 15

Happy Ending

I always wanted God to give me a happy ending . . . to tie it in a bow just perfect. Just like the movies, I desired the "and they lived happily ever after." But again, that's only the ending of the *story*. It's the end of the *movie*. In reality, it's just the beginning. What if we viewed our lives that way? What if God wants to give you your bow in the middle? What if He wants to take your life, wrap it up in a bow and gift you your happily ever after in the middle—of the mess, of the journey, of life? He wants to redeem your heart and satisfy your soul. And that is where life begins. Life begins with the happily ever after, and what if He wants to give it to you right now?

||||||||||||||||||||||||||||||||||||||||||||||||||||||||||||||||||||||||||||||||||||||||||||||||||

He wants to redeem your heart and satisfy your soul. And that is where life begins.

||||||||||||||||||||||||||||||||||||||||||||||||||||||||||||||||||||||||||||||||||||||||||||||||||

People always say life is about the journey. I've really been more focused on the endgame. I like to know concrete facts. I've wanted to make sure I get to the end, and in the process, I've missed a lot of life. But what if we could have the "happily ever after" ending, secure, safe, and fully assured in the middle?

That's exactly what Christ gives us, an assurance, and we don't have to wait until the end. He will meet you there—in the middle. He's the bow. He's the hope. He is the redeemer of your soul . . . your knight in shining armor. The bow isn't perfect circumstances—we're not guaranteed those on earth, and we know we will all face trials. "Happily ever after," the bow that I want on top of all of it is this:

God created me, He saw me, He knows all of me, and He still wanted me. He saved me, forgave me, redeemed me, remade me, and restored His gracious relationship with me. He's the love that I've always longed for, and the amazing part is—He found me in the middle.

The story continues . . . as does life. This time, though, I'm enjoying the journey, not looking to the end. I know I already have it (His love/forgiveness/life), so I'm looking to the now.

Being.

Yielding, submitting, obeying, trusting, resting.

It's up and down. I am still working through all of these at different times. Yes, God is gracious with me and faithful to me. My hope for you is Psalm 16:11(ESV): "You make known to me the path of life; in your presence, there is fullness of joy; at your right hand are pleasures forevermore."

I pray that you learn the practice of being. Being at rest. Being in a relationship with God. Being present. Being who He created you to be. I pray you would find joy in HIS presence. That the love you so desperately long for is found in Jesus. I pray you would open your heart to Him . . . and He will lead you to truth, healing, wholeness, and life. I pray that you would find the lover of your soul in Jesus. It's not like the movies; it's much better.

"The Lord your God is with you,
the Mighty Warrior who saves.
He will take great delight in you;
in his love he will no longer rebuke you,
but will rejoice over you with singing." —Zephaniah 3:17 (NIV)

You are loved.

Appendix A

Bible Verses on Identity in Christ

I am loved.

» "I have loved you with an everlasting love; I have drawn you with unfailing kindness."(Jeremiah 31:3, NIV)

» "For God so loved the world that he gave his one and only son, that whosoever believes in him will have eternal life." (John 3:16, NIV)

I am a child of God. I am accepted.

» "But to all who did receive him, who believed in his name, he gave the right to become children of God." (John 1:12, ESV)

» "See what great love the Father lavished on us, that we should be called the children of God! And that is what we are! The reason the world does not know us is that it did not know him." (1 John 3:1, NIV)

» "And I will be your Father, and you will be my sons and daughters, says the LORD Almighty." (2 Corinthians 6:18, NLT)

» "So in Christ Jesus you are all children of God through faith." (Galatians 3:26, NIV)

I am uniquely created.

» "So, God created mankind in his own image, in the image of God, he created them; male and female he created them." (Genesis 1:27, NIV)

» "For we are God's masterpiece. He has created us anew in Christ Jesus, so we can do the good things he planned for us long ago." (Ephesians 2:10, NLT)

» "For you created my inmost being; you knit me together in my mother's womb. I praise you because I am fearfully and wonderfully made; your works are wonderful, I know that full well." (Psalm 139:13-14, NIV)

God is with me. I am not alone.

» "Do you not know that your bodies are temples of the Holy Spirit, who is in you, whom you have received from God?" (1 Corinthians 6:19, NIV)

» "And I will ask the Father, and he will give you another advocate to help you and be with you forever—the spirit of truth." (John14:16-17, NIV)

» "The Lord your God is with you, the Mighty Warrior who saves. He will take great delight in you; in his love, he will no longer rebuke you, but will rejoice over you with singing." (Zephaniah 3:17, NIV)

» "Be strong and courageous. Do not be afraid or terrified because of them, for the LORD your God goes with you; he will never leave you nor forsake you." (Deuteronomy 31:6, NIV)

I am made new.

» "But now you must also rid yourselves of all such things as these: anger, rage, malice, slander, and filthy language from your lips. Do not lie to each other, since you have taken off your old self with its practices and have put on the new self, which is being renewed in knowledge in the image of its Creator." (Colossians 3:8-10, NIV)

» "Therefore, if anyone is in Christ, the new creation has come: The old has gone, the new is here!" (2 Corinthians 5:17, NIV)

I am strong.

» I am "strengthened with all might according to his glorious power." (Colossians 1:11, KJV)

» "I can do all things through Christ who strengthens me." (Philippians 4:13, NKJV)

» "Have I not commanded you? Be strong and courageous. Do not be afraid; do not be discouraged, for the Lord your God will be with you wherever you go." (Joshua 1:9, NIV)

» "God is our refuge and strength, an ever-present help in trouble." (Psalm 46:1, NIV)

» "But He has said to me, 'My grace is sufficient for you [My lovingkindness and My mercy are more than enough—always available—regardless of the situation]; for [My] power is being perfected [and is completed and shows itself most effectively] in [your] weakness.' Therefore, I will all the more gladly boast in my weaknesses, so that the power of Christ [may completely enfold me and] may dwell in me." (2 Corinthians 12:9, AMP)

» "Strength and dignity are her clothing, *and* her position is strong and secure; And she smiles at the future [knowing that she and her family are prepared]." (Proverbs 31:25, AMP)

» "The Lord is my strength and my shield; in him my heart trusts, and I am helped; my heart exults, and with my song, I give thanks to him." (Psalm 28:7, ESV)

» "He gives power to the faint, and to him who has no might, he increases strength. Even youths shall faint and be weary, and young men shall fall exhausted; but they who wait for the Lord shall renew their strength; they shall mount up with wings like eagles; they shall run and not be weary; they shall walk and not faint." (Isaiah 40:29-31, ESV)

» "Fear not, for I am with you; be not dismayed, for I am your God; I will strengthen you, I will help you, I will uphold you with my righteous right hand." (Isaiah 41:10, ESV)

I am secure.

» "And we know that in all things God works for the good of those who love him, who have been called according to his purpose." (Romans 8:28, NIV)

» "And those whom he predestined he also called, and those whom he called he also justified, and those whom he justified he also glorified. What then shall we say to these things? If God is for us, who can be against us? He who did not spare his own Son but gave him up for us all, how will he not also with him graciously give us all things?" (Romans 8:30-32, ESV)

» "Do not fear [anything], for I am with you; Do not be afraid, for I am your God. I will strengthen you, be assured I will help you; I will certainly take hold of you with My righteous right hand [a hand of justice, of power, of victory, of salvation]." (Isaiah 41:10, AMP)

I am forgiven.

» "In Him we have redemption through his blood, the forgiveness of sins, in accordance with the riches of God's grace." (Ephesians 1:7, NIV)

» "If we confess our sins, he is faithful and just to forgive us our sins and to cleanse us from all unrighteousness." (1 John 1:9, ESV)

» We are delivered from the power of darkness and translated into God's kingdom. (Colossians 1:13, author paraphrase)
» I am the righteousness of God through Christ Jesus. (2 Corinthians 5:21, author paraphrase)

Appendix B

What is all this talk about God's love?

Whether this is the first time or the hundredth time you have heard about God's love for you, I want to stop and take a moment for you to respond. You might see this love, forgiveness, and gift that God is offering and be thinking, *Well, not me; you don't know what I've done or what's been done to me. I'm too broken, too far gone.* Or maybe you have heard about God's love one hundred times and don't know how to say, *Yes, God, I want You in my life.* I want to tell you that I've been there. We all have, and the truth is, yes, God loves you. All of you. If you feel broken, rejected, lost, or even indifferent, God sees you, and He is willing to meet you where you are. You don't need to be perfect to come to God—actually quite the opposite. Romans 5:8 (NIV) says, "But God demonstrates his own love for us in this: While we were still sinners, Christ died for us." God loved you first, before you even knew you needed Him, before you even asked. God sent Jesus because He loved us.

Here is a simple prayer to start you on your journey and to say yes to God.

Heavenly Father,

Thank You for loving me. Thank You for the gift of grace. I know that I am a sinner; I fall short. I no longer want to live in sin or my own strength. Please come into my heart, mind, body, and spirit. Forgive me for my sins, cleanse me, and make me new. Heal my broken heart. Lead me, Jesus. Be my guide and Lord. Amen

If you prayed that prayer, all of heaven is celebrating with you, and so am I. Believe me; this will be the greatest decision you will ever make in your life. Setting your foundation and identity on this solid foundation of God's love for you is the safest place to live. I prayed that prayer thirty years ago as a child, and I'm so thankful to have been raised learning the truth. But honestly, the day I decided to live this out and accept Jesus as my Lord and allow Him to be my foundation was in 2018. Since then, my life has been radically changed; I've been made new. God is faithful. He was faithful to me throughout my childhood and faithful to bring me to a deeper understanding of His love and truth as an adult. God is with you and will be faithful to bring you through, too.

CPSIA information can be obtained
at www.ICGtesting.com
Printed in the USA
BVHW032127251122
652777BV00016B/1008